You are to prepare for the
invasion of Europe, for
unless we can go and land
and fight Hitler and beat
his forces on land, we
shall never win this war.
                    -- Winston Churchill
                         October 1941

In the last great invasion...

Of the last great war...

The greatest danger for eight men...

...was saving one.

saving private ryan

The Men. The Mission. The Movie.

A Film by Steven Spielberg

Photographs by David James

NEWMARKET PRESS • NEW YORK

Design and compilation copyright © 1998 by Newmarket Press.

Page 17 Text used with permission from *The 101st Airborne at Normandy*
by Mark Bando and published by MB! Publishing, Osceola, Wisconsin.

Pages 15, 19, 21, 22 Text reprinted with the permission of Simon &
Schuster, Inc. from *D-Day: June 6, 1944, The Climactic Battle of World
War II* by Stephen E. Ambrose. New York: Simon & Schuster, 1994.
Copyright © 1994 by Ambrose-Tubbs, Inc. All Rights Reserved.

Pages 28, 33, 36 Text reprinted with the permission of Simon &
Schuster, Inc. from *Citizen Soldiers: The U.S. Army from the Normandy
Beaches to the Bulge to the Surrender of Germany June 7, 1944– May 7,
1945* by Stephen E. Ambrose. New York: Simon & Schuster, 1997.
Copyright © 1997 by Ambrose-Tubbs Inc. All Rights Reserved.

Pages 24-5, 29, 31 *Voices of D-Day: The Story of the Allied Invasion
Told by Those Who Were There.* Edited by Ronald J. Drez. Baton Rouge:
Louisiana State University Press, 1994. Copyright © 1994 by The
Eisenhower Center for Leadership Studies. All Rights Reserved.

10 9 8 7 6 5 4 3 2 1

ISBN: 1-55704-370-1 (hc); 1-55704-371-X (pb)

Library of Congress Cataloging-in-Publication Data
is available upon request.

 Published by Newmarket Press • New York

This book is published simultaneously in
the United States and in Canada.

Quantity Purchases
Companies, professional groups, clubs, and other organizations may
qualify for special terms when ordering quantities of this title. For
information, write Special Sales, Newmarket Press, 18 East 48th Street,
New York, NY 10017, call (212) 832-3575, or fax (212) 832-3629.

Edited by Linda Sunshine.

Design by Timothy Shaner, Night & Day Design.

DreamWorks Project Executive: Jerry Schmitz
DreamWorks Photo Editor: Boyd Peterson
DreamWorks Art Director: Randy Nellis

Produced by Newmarket Productions, a division of Newmarket
Publishing and Communications Company: Esther Margolis, director;
Keith Hollaman, editor; Frank DeMaio, production manager.

Manufactured in the United States of America
First Edition

INTRODUCTION

Set during and immediately following the invasion of Normandy, *Saving Private Ryan* tells the story of a squad of American soldiers on a dangerous mission to find Private James Ryan whose three brothers have been killed in combat. On direct orders from Washington, Captain John Miller leads his men deep behind enemy lines. As the squad pushes on, the men find themselves asking: Why is one man worth risking the lives of eight?

Amid the chaos and terror of those days in early June 1944, this remarkable story searches to find decency in the sheer madness of war.

While preparing to film *Saving Private Ryan*, hundreds of people spent countless hours researching and re-creating the battles, the landscape, and the destruction of France during those days. One thousand soldiers were employed in filming the landing on Omaha Beach. Original landing boats, guns, and gear were restored to working order. While shooting the battle scenes in strict chronological order, tens of thousands of rounds of ammunition were fired. Every effort was made to capture the harsh reality of war as authentically as possible.

World War II was perhaps the pivotal event of the twentieth century and a defining moment for America and the world. It shifted the borders of the globe, forever changed those who survived it, and shaped the past five decades.

D - D A Y

All draftees gained a lot more muscle after thirteen weeks of training.

The U.S. Army's infantry divisions were not distinguished by any outstanding characteristics.

The Selective Service System was just that, selective. Originally, of the men called to service were rejected after physical examinations, making the average draftee brighter, healthier, and better-educated than the average American. He was twenty-six years old, five feet eight inches tall, weighed 144 pounds, had a thirty-three-and-a-half-inch chest, and a thirty-one-inch waist. After thirteen weeks of basic training, he'd gained seven pounds (and converted many of his original pounds from fat to muscle) and added at least an inch to his chest. Nearly half the draftees were high-school graduates; one in ten had some college. As Geoffrey Perret puts it in his history of the U.S. Army in World War II, "These were the best-educated enlisted men of any army in history."

At the end of 1943 the U.S. Army was the greenest army in the world. Of the nearly fifty infantry, armored, and airborne divisions selected for participation in the campaign in northwest Europe, only two—the 1st Infantry and the 82nd Airborne—had been in combat.

This posed problems and caused apprehension, but it had a certain advantage. According to Pvt. Carl Weast of the U.S. 5th Ranger Battalion, "A veteran infantryman is a terrified infantryman." Sgt. Carwood Lipton of the 506th Parachute Infantry Regiment (PIR) of the 101st Airborne commented, "I took chances on D-Day I would never have taken later in the war."

"A veteran infantryman is a terrified infantryman."
Theme

positions. Booby traps, shells, bullets, or land mines—to say nothing of mortar fire—did do real human body are terrifying to men who have seen the carnage. Men in their late teens or early twenties have a feeling of invulnerability as seen in the words of Charles East of the 29th Division. Told by his commanding officer, on the eve of D-Day, that nine out of ten would become casualties in the ensuing campaign, East looked at the man to his left, then to the man on his right, and thought to himself, "You poor bastards."

D-Day: June 6, 1944
The Climactic Battle of World War II
by Stephen E. Ambrose

The Men.

June 6, 1944

OFFICE OF THE REGIMENTAL COMMANDER

Soldiers of the _____ D-Day

Today, and as y___ _____ this, you
are en route t_ _____ _____ _____
for which you _____ _____ ___ ____
two years.

Tonight is the _____ _____ __ _____

Tomorrow thro_____ the whole of ___r
homeland and _____ Allied world the
bells will ri__ __ ___ ____ ___ that
you have arri___ _____ _____
for liberation has begun.

The hopes and prayers of your dear
ones accompany you, the confidence
of your high commanders goes with
you. The fears of the Germans are
about to become a reality.

Let us strike hard. When the going is
tough, let us go harder. Imbued with
faith in the rightness of our cause,
and the power of our might, let us
annihilate the enemy where found.

May God be with each of you fine
soldiers. By your actions let us
justify His faith in us.

Colonel Robert Sink
(Memo to his 506th Troopers)

"en real route to that great adventure for which you have trained for over two years." irony

People of Western
Europe: A landing
was made this morning
on the coast of
France by troops
of the Allied
Expeditionary Force...

...I call upon all who
love freedom to stand
with us now. Together we
shall achieve victory.
-- Dwight D. Eisenhower
Broadcast on D-Day

Lt. Den Brotheridge fired a full clip of thirty-two rounds from his Sten gun. Those were the first shots fired by the 175,000 British, American, Canadian, Free French, Polish, Norwegian, and other nationalities in the Allied Expeditionary Force set to invade Normandy in the next twenty-four hours.
                                    -- Stephen E. Ambrose, D-Day

So the GI hitting the beach in the first wave at Omaha would have to get through the minefields in the Channel without his LST blowing up, then get from ship to shore in a Higgins boat taking fire from inland batteries, then work his way through an obstacle-studded tidal flat of some 150 meters crisscrossed by machine gun and rifle fire, with big shells whistling by and mortars exploding all around, to find his first protection behind the shingle. There he would be caught in a triple crossfire—machine guns and heavy artillery from the sides, small arms from the front, mortars coming down from above.

-- Stephen E. Ambrose, D-Day

About seven or eight in the morning, we were being urged by braver and more sensible noncoms and one or two surviving officers to get off the beach and up the bluffs to higher ground. More men from other landing craft behind us were making it across the beach and joining the congestion at the seawall. It would be some time before enough courage returned for us to attempt movement up the slopes and up the beach. Scared, worried, and often praying, I had been busy helping some of the wounded; most of the time, moving in

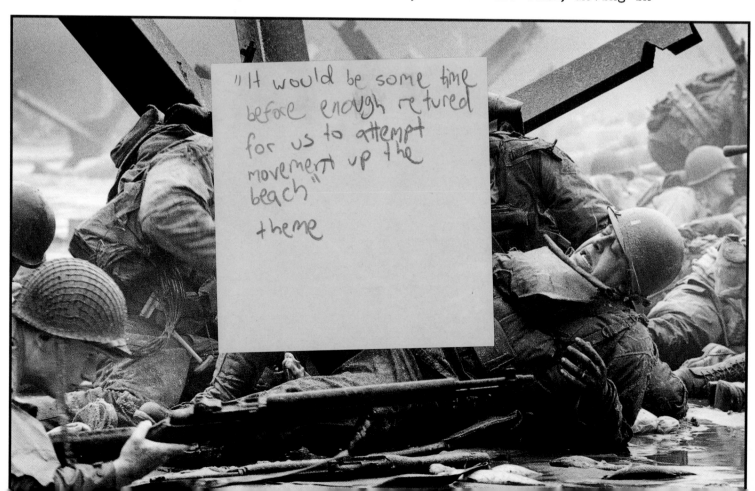

"It would be some time before enough retured for us to attempt movement up the beach"

theme

a crouched position, a few of us helped move the helpless to
secure areas. Once or twice I was able to control my fear enough
to race across the sand to drag a helpless GI from drowning in the
incoming tide. That was the extent of my bravery that morning. Then
clear thinking replaced some of our fear, and many of us accepted
the fact that we had to get off the beach or die where we were.
We got off the beach.

                -- Harry Parley, Private First Class, Company E, from Voices of D-Day

Normandy was a soldier's battle. It belonged to the riflemen, machine gunners, mortarmen, tankers, and artillery men who were on the front lines. There was no room for maneuver. There was no opportunity for subtlety. There was a simplicity to the fighting: for the Germans, to hold; for the Americans, to attack.

-- Stephen E. Ambrose, *Citizen Soldiers*

As ranking noncom, I tried to get my men off the boat and make it somehow to the cliff, but it was horrible--men frozen in the sand, unable to move. My radio man had his head blown off three yards from me. The beach was covered with bodies--men with no legs, no arms--God, it was awful. It was absolutely terrible.

 -- Harry Bare, Sergeant, Company F, 1st Squadron, from Voices of D-Day

"I tried to get my men off the boat and make it somehow to the cliff, but it was horrible—men frozen in the sand, unable to move." —them

There was thousands of ships, and we could see landing
boats of American troops. Then came thousands of men at
one time coming on land and running over the beach.
This is the first time I shoot on living men, and
I go to the machine gun and I shoot, I shoot,
I shoot! For each American I see fall,
there came ten hundred other ones!
-- Franz Rachmann, Private,
German 352nd Division,
from Voices of D-Day

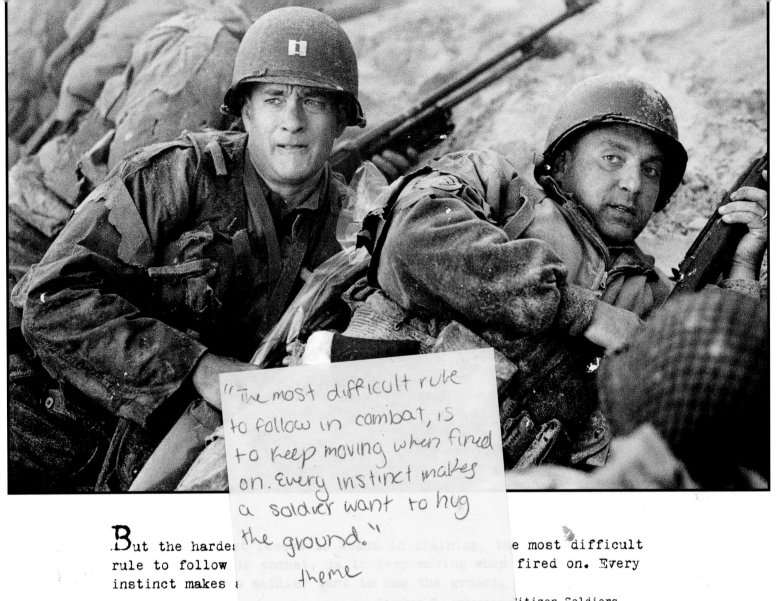

"The most difficult rule to follow in combat, is to keep moving when fired on. Every instinct makes a soldier want to hug the ground."

theme

But the hardest lesson to teach in training, the most difficult rule to follow in combat, is to keep moving when fired on. Every instinct makes a soldier want to hug the ground.

—Stephen E. Ambrose, Citizen Soldiers

By June 30, the Americans had brought 71,000 vehicles over the beaches (of a planned 110,000) and 452,000 soldiers (of a planned 579,000)...It had eleven divisions in the battle, as scheduled, plus the 82nd and the 101st Airborne... The Americans had evacuated 27,000 casualties. About 11,000 GIs had been killed in action or died of their wounds, 1,000 were missing in action, and 3,400 wounded men had been returned to duty. So the total active duty strength of U.S. First Army in Normandy on June 30 was 413,000. German strength on the American front was somewhat less, while German losses against the combined British-Canadian-American forces were 47,500.

-- Stephen E. Ambrose, <u>Citizen Soldiers</u>

The Mission.

29 ON MILLER

Miller and the others look around, stunned -- we did it. We're alive. After the beach, it's more than any of them expected. Nobody says anything, because there really aren't words to express the moment. We're here. It's a fact.

Sarge reaches down, picks up a handful of sand, and pours it into a container that is already premarked "France." He screws the tin lid back on and puts it back in his pack next to two similar tin cans upon which are crudely inscribed in smeared blue ink "Africa" and "Italy."

--from the screenplay

Corporal Upham

Sergeant Horvath

Private Jackson

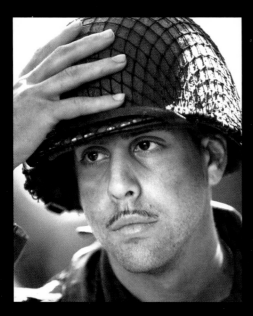

Private Mellish

ON MILLER AND REIBEN

        REIBEN
This goes against every-
thing the army taught me.
Makes no sense—

        MILLER
What doesn't make sense,
Reiben?

        REIBEN
The math, sir. Of this
mission. Maybe you could
explain it to me.

        MILLER
What do you want to
know?

        REIBEN
Well, sir, in purely
arithmetic terms, what's
the sense in risking eight
guys to save one?

Private Caparzo

Private Reiben

T/4 Medic Wade

Captain Miller

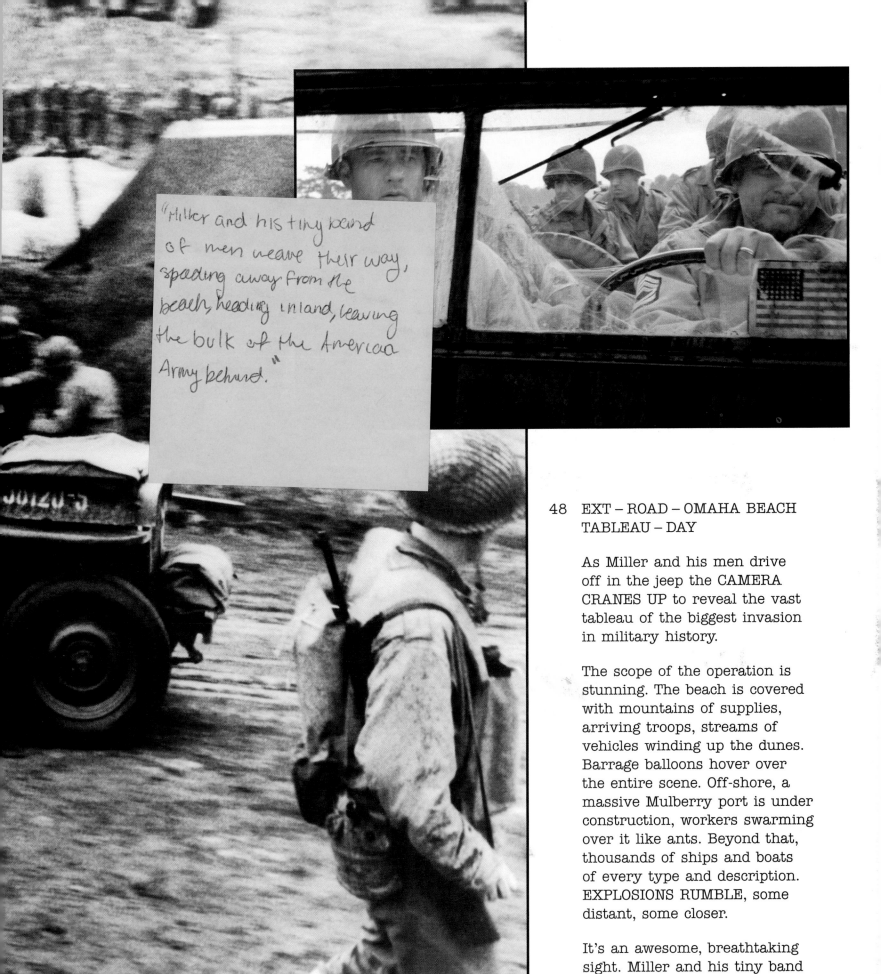

"Miller and his tiny band of men weave their way, speeding away from the beach, heading inland, leaving the bulk of the American Army behind."

48   EXT – ROAD – OMAHA BEACH
      TABLEAU – DAY

As Miller and his men drive off in the jeep the CAMERA CRANES UP to reveal the vast tableau of the biggest invasion in military history.

The scope of the operation is stunning. The beach is covered with mountains of supplies, arriving troops, streams of vehicles winding up the dunes. Barrage balloons hover over the entire scene. Off-shore, a massive Mulberry port is under construction, workers swarming over it like ants. Beyond that, thousands of ships and boats of every type and description. EXPLOSIONS RUMBLE, some distant, some closer.

It's an awesome, breathtaking sight. Miller and his tiny band of men weave their way, speeding away from the beach, heading inland, leaving the bulk of the American Army behind.

54   EXT.   HEDGEROW CART ROAD – DAY

Miller walks point. His men follow warily. It's hot. They're
exhausted. Upham looks miserable, weighed down like a pack
horse with all the B.A.R. ammunition, slapping at horseflies.
They talk quietly, their eyes scanning.

UPHAM
"War educates the senses, calls into action the will, perfects the
physical constitution, brings men into such swift and close collision
in critical moments that man measures man."

MILLER
I guess that's Emerson's way to look on the bright side.

CAPARZO
Captain. Decent thing to do would be to at least take the kids
down the road to the next town.

MILLER
We're not here to do the decent thing, Caparzo. We're here to
follow orders.

Miller watches his men go. He gives himself
a second and looks at what remains of the
once lovely village, now nothing more than
rubble. Hamill steps up next to him. Though
strangers, Miller and Hamill speak like tired
old friends.

                HAMILL (CONT'D)
        What do you hear? How's it all
        falling together?

                MILLER
        Beachhead's secure but it's slow
        goin'. Monty's takin' his time
        getting to Caen, we can't move
        'til he's ready.

                HAMILL
        That guy's over-rated.

                MILLER
        No kiddin'.

Hamill shakes his head and sighs.

                HAMILL
        We gotta take Caen to take St. Lo.

                MILLER
        And we gotta take St. Lo to take
        Valognes.

                HAMILL
        Gotta take Valognes to take
        Cherbourg.

                MILLER
        Gotta take Cherbourg to take
        Paris.

                HAMILL
        Gotta take Paris to take Berlin.

                MILLER
        Gotta take Berlin to take a boat
        home.

MILLER
Every time you kill one of your men, you
tell yourself you just saved the lives of
two, three, ten, a hundred others. You
know how many men I've lost under
my command?

SARGE
How many?

MILLER
(instantly)
Ninety-four. So that must mean I've
saved the lives of ten times that number.
Maybe twenty, right? See it's simple.
It lets you always choose the mission
over men.

SARGE
Except this time the mission is a man.

Miller looks at Sarge now. His eyes hard.

MILLER
And Ryan better be worth it. He better
go home and cure some disease or invent
a new longer-lasting lightbulb.

MILLER
Tell me, Reiben, you had to do it again, how'd you think you'd react the next time?

REIBEN
Me? I'd shoot myself 'fore I ever got off the damn boat.

Ryan stands, indicates the other guys in his unit.

RYAN (CONT'D)
Hell, these guys deserve to go home as much
as I do. They've fought just as hard.

MILLER
Is that what I'm supposed to tell your mother,
she gets another flag?

RYAN
You can tell her that when you found me, I
was with the only brothers I had left. And that
there was no way I was deserting them. I think
she'd understand that.

He and Miller stare at each other.

SARGE

I don't know. Part of me thinks the kid's right, he asks what he's done to deserve this. He wants to stay here, fine. Let's leave him and go home. But then another part of me thinks what if by some miracle we stay then actually make it out of here. Someday we might look back on this and decide that saving Private Ryan was the one decent thing we were able to pull out of this whole godawful mess. Like you said, Capt'n, maybe we do that, we <u>all</u> earn the right to go home.

118   ANGLE ON STREET

—and thunderous hell breaks loose as the HAWKINS MINES
DETONATE massively along both sides of the street. The walls
blow out towards the infantry, taking them down with
concussion and shrapnel, killing at least a dozen men...

The MACHINE GUNS OPEN FIRE at the same moment, turning
the street into a killing zone

156 THE LAST SANDBAG EMPLACEMENT

... and then the Tiger FIRES ITS CANNON. THE EXPLOSION TEARS THE WORLD APART, spinning it upside-down, ripping the air with heat and shrapnel...

... and everything goes quiet, as if the sound has drained out of the world. We're left with sounds that are remote, faint, surreal, disembodied...

158 RESUME NORMAL SPEED AND SOUND:

...as a P-51 MUSTANG swoops grandly over the bridge. Tank-buster. It peels overhead, no longer with the sound of voices but with a THROATY ROAR OF A PACKARD ENGINE.

The Movie.

Although I admire war movies and have seen many of them, I wasn't really looking to make a World War II film. I didn't want to shoot the picture as a Hollywood gung-ho Rambo kind of extravaganza. I wanted the audience to be fairly uneasy sitting through the invasion of Normandy.

Our approach to the movie was the way a documentary filmmaker would have approached it in, for example, John Ford's unit shooting the South Pacific War or George Stevens's unit shooting the European campaign. We just had a camera. Janusz stripped all the glossy filters and the filaments from the lenses so they were just like the kind of lenses they actually used in the Second World War. We shot a lot of the war sequences with the shutter speed used by those Bell and Howell cameras of the 1940s for making newsreels.

The audience won't feel much difference except, if we've done our jobs, they will think we were actually on the beach on D-Day.
                                    —Steven Spielberg

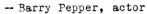

The actors in boot camp.
(Left to right) Front row: Barry Pepper, Tom Hanks, Tom Sizemore, Ed Burns, Capt. Dale Dye, Adam Goldberg, Giovanni Ribisi, Jeremy Davies. Back row: Assistants to Dale Dye.

We went through an extensive training period in the woods for the better part of a week, which helped us understand about the gear and what it's like to slog this stuff around. We're essentially playing guys who are tired and miserable and want to go home. Great physical demands are being made of them constantly.

We hiked all over the place; it was rainy and cold and wet. We slept on the ground and ate food that came out of cans, heated up over little tiny stoves. Dale was constantly yelling at us because we were doing things wrong. We learned various combat techniques but that wasn't as important as the experience itself.

We were up at five in the morning, carrying very heavy stuff on our backs all day long, and we only had a few moments to lie down in the grass and maybe go to sleep. But then we had to get up again; the day's not over until two in the morning.

Now we do that in microcosm as actors, but all of us will tell you that we couldn't have played our parts without experiencing what Dale Dye put us through.

—Tom Hanks

Basic Training

"I'm like the guy in On the Waterfront"

simile

I'm not a wilderness guy. I mean, I'm like the guy in *On the Waterfront* who says, "The crickets make me nervous." I'm a very New York guy. And so already, sleeping out in the wilderness is a stretch for me. And then to sleep under harsh rain conditions and be woken up after only a few hours following a really hard day—it was very rough.

But it did serve two functions. One was the brotherhood. There could not have been a more bonding experience. The other is that our relationship with Tom Hanks couldn't have been set up any better. Every single guy in the platoon wanted to leave early except for Tom who was the only one who said we should stay an extra few days. And it was so appropriate because he's playing the Captain who has the most endurance.

— Vin Diesel, actor

I didn't want to go to boot camp. I'm an actor, I'm going to *act* like a marine, why do I have to *be* a marine? It's called acting, not "being."

We were taken to this forest and given a blanket, no pillow. It was hard to sleep on the ground! In L.A., I don't sleep on the ground, I sleep in a bed.

We got up at four in the morning and ran five miles and did all these push-ups and sit-ups. You don't eat anything and your feet stick out of the tent at night! And since I'm the Sarge, I have to walk around and kick the guys in the feet to wake them up in the morning.

This is nuts, but we really went through something like the men in the movie experienced. In the field, the men would go to their sergeant to voice their grievances and then the sarge went to the captain and that's how it happened in our boot camp. The other actors, Eddie Burns, Vin Diesel, Adam Goldberg, and Jeremy Davies, would come to me to say, "I can't do this."

But then something happened to all of us. We really learned that no one does anything alone in a war. It's all about teamwork—if the other guy's sick or can't get his gear on, you stop and help him out. That's what the marines are all about—it's a brotherhood. We got just a taste of that and it brought us closer together so that when we started shooting we felt a bond.

Still, after boot camp, the first thing I did was drink a Diet Coke.

—Tom Sizemore, actor

Top: **Boot camp.**
Left: (Left to right) Tom Hanks, Capt. Dale Dye, Vin Diesel, Tom Sizemore.

"Captain Dye only referred to us by our character names. It was sort of like Stanislavsky running boot camp."
--Adam Goldberg, actor

We spent a week together living out in the woods in tents. It was the worst experience of my life. It really was. It was physically exhausting and tough; it was really hard on all of us. But we got a real sense of what these guys went through.

We spent a lot of time talking with Captain Dye, who'd been in Vietnam and Desert Storm. Every night we'd ask him questions about his experiences. What was your relationship with the guys you're serving with? What was it like to lose a friend? And how terrifying was it when you were behind enemy lines and walking around at night in the woods without being able to see five feet in front of you? What's going on in your head?

—Ed Burns, actor

"Steven says, 'Real is the watchword,' and if it looks horrible on screen, well, so it is in combat. The more horrible we can show it, the more people will understand the nobility of the sacrifice that those men made."
--Capt. Dale Dye, USMC (ret.)

"Actors-who are like dry sponges until you pour on the water" simile

Omaha Beach scene.
(Left to right) Tom Sanders, Production Designer; Steven Spielberg, Director; Tom Hanks, Actor; Capt. Dale Dye, Senior Military Advisor.

I believe there is a certain core spirit within an American fighting man, within a fighting man of any nationality. A certain heart and spirit is common with all fighting men. Actors—who are like dry sponges until you pour on the water—need to be immersed in the rigorous lifestyle, in the horrors facing infantrymen and combat people all over the world. So to the extent that insurance and lifestyles will allow, I immerse those actors in that lifestyle. I take them to the field, I make them eat rations, I shoot at them with blank ammunition, I beat them up, I beat on them, I make them crawl and sleep in the mud and the cold and the dirt. And when they come out the other end, if I've done my job successfully, they have an inkling of what it's like—the deprivations, the hardships people endure to serve their country in the military.
—Capt. Dale Dye, USMC (ret.)

For locations, I looked all around France, Ireland, and England. Ireland had an area that looked exactly like Normandy. The landscape and the beaches were so similar it was uncanny.

We had to have beach access, so we were also looking for a place with a harbor. We needed a particular kind of tide to have a certain amount of beach left when the tide was in, for the crew on the beach.

Also, we needed a location where we could house a thousand-man army and a 45-man crew.

Having worked in Ireland before, we knew we could hire its army, which was a key element. Without a trained army to jump out of the boats and storm the beach with experience, we'd have to train a lot of extras. We needed regiments. We had to get them ready every day and have them on the set.

Logistically, it was a nightmare.

—Tom Sanders, production designer

Crew members on the beach in Ireland.
(Left to right) Steve Painter, Make-up Effects Artist; Mitch Dubin, Camera Operator; Maxie McDonald, Prop Master; Jim Kwiatkowski, Key Grip; Neil Corbould, Special Effects; Janusz Kaminski, Director of Photography; Steven Spielberg, Director; Ian Bryce, Producer; Sergio Mimica, First Assistant Director; Chris Haarhoff, Steadi-Cam/Camera Operator; Lisa Dean Kavanaugh, Set Decorator.

The tanks and other vehicles were fairly easy to find but not the landing craft. We found some in England and a couple in Scotland, but, interestingly enough, the majority of them were in Palm Springs, California.

We bought them and built cradles to ship them over. They arrived in Southampton and we sent them to a refurbishing yard. Then we put them on another ship and sent them to Ireland. It was a pretty big moving operation for the transportation department.

There are twelve of these landing craft in the movie and several hundred in the background.
—Ian Bryce, producer

One day we were out there on the boats and the Irish sea was really rough. It was a cold, stormy day and the Higgins boats were slamming pretty hard, bouncing and pounding through the surf; the chop was like four to five feet swells. A few of the guys around me were getting sick. We were getting really upset, as in reality, not our characters. We were just very nervous about the water and being in the boats and we got this incredible feeling of impending doom.

It gave me this minute sensation of what it must've been like out there. It was really scary for me. My mind just started to wander and think about how afraid these young guys must have been. And they were so tired and soaking wet. They had all their layers of wool clothing and all their gear and ammunition and when they stepped off the boat, they saw all their pals dying around them. They were so exhausted and seasick and all they could do was crawl up those beaches. And thousands of them lay dead in no time at all. It's unthinkable.

—Barry Pepper, actor

It took us three months to gather the 2,000 weapons that we used in the film. About 500 of them were capable of firing blanks, the others were rubber. They all needed dusting, cleaning, and painting each evening.

We brought them all from England. Some of our weapons came from Germany, but a lot of the American artillery is in England.

Of course, we had to deactivate certain weapons and make sure they weren't capable of firing live ammunition.

—Simon Atherton, armourer

First, I respond emotionally to what the film should look like; the words go through my heart and then I try to put them on the screen.

There were many parallels between this movie and *Schindler's List*. Both were World War II dramas that I envisioned in a semi-documentary style, using hand-held cameras for images that were full of texture. My other idea was to subtract some of the color from the film in a desaturation process done after the movie is shot. About

sixty percent of the color was extracted from the final negative.

I didn't want blue skies, I didn't want any clouds. Through the whole course of the movie, there's virtually not a single shot of blue sky. I was going for this kind of burned-out, bleary sky, and I used various techniques to achieve these visuals. For example, Panavision in Los Angeles prepared a particular set of lenses for me. They extracted the protective coating inside the lens so the images were slightly more defused and prone to flares, and the skies were burned out. The whole image was softer without being out of focus.

Another technique was that we used a different shadow degree to achieve a certain staccato in the actors' movement. We got a crispness of explosions. Everything we shot became slightly, just slightly, more realistic.

—Janusz Kaminski, cinematographer

We're at Hatfield Aerodrome, which is north of London. When we started here, this was a grass field. We decided that it would be better to build a river for environmental reasons and for control. We started from scratch, dug the river back here, and put in the bridge.

We had to build these buildings because we couldn't find anything like this in Europe. It's all historically accurate.

After three trips to France, we built a model of a French village. We made this whole town in model form and then we slowly carved out the places where the bombs would've hit.

The model for this whole town took us five weeks to build in Los Angeles and then we shipped it over here. It's a great tool for the director and the cinematographer to use. They see the set-up in color and in three dimensions.

—Tom Sanders,
production designer

Following page: **Aerial view of the set at Hatfield Aerodrome, which was formerly a grass field.**

Many years ago I was working as a bellman in a hotel, and the guy who picked up the dry cleaning every afternoon and brought it back in the morning was a D-Day veteran. He was away on vacation for two weeks, and when he returned I asked him how it went. He said, "Well, it was both good and it was bad."

He told me that he was a veteran of the 101st Airborne, the paratroopers who jumped on June 5th. Every year he went to this reunion. But every year there were fewer and fewer guys among the group of survivors.

As soon as I read the script for *Saving Private Ryan*, he was one of the first guys who came to my mind.

As a film subject, World War II, by and large, is a never-ending, fascinating lesson for an actor. There was so much about the invasion of Europe that translates in actor's terms: motivations and movement, even the props and costumes.

We started this movie with the utter chaos and shambles of Omaha Beach, which really put everything in its proper perspective. We had lines we never even shot. It was a waste of time to try and establish any kind of rapport amongst us after all the carnage we witnessed.

If we hadn't started with D-Day, and I think Steven would probably agree, we would've wasted an awful lot of time trying to establish other stuff that wasn't important. After D-Day the whole point was: Let's find this guy and get home.

There are a lot of brilliant World War II movies, but it's been thirty years since a real chronicle epic of the war has been made.

For our generation who grew up on various World War II movies, I think that war has a kind of mythical memory connected to being kids and having fathers who were in the war as well as the influence of all those television shows and movies. For the younger generation, it's ancient history. They probably think Normandy is a country right next to Sweden.

Still, we don't want to lecture an audience. We are trying to communicate to them that mere mortals, people who are the same age as themselves, had to be called upon to make this hard sacrifice in service to mankind. From a purely humanistic point of view, I think it's important to go back and examine this piece of history.

—Tom Hanks, actor

Any scene involving the characters as they explore their fragilities are the ones that surprise me the most. I knew that the invasion scenes would work because Steven Spielberg is so accurate about the military and technical aspects. The D-Day landing is very startling, very dramatic, but it's not surprising. But when the actors and the director bring the smaller moments to life, that's when I get startled and I say, "Hey, I didn't write that. Great!"

— Robert Rodat, screenwriter

As a young director observing Spielberg's approach to directing, I've noticed that he's like an undefeated boxer who is so good that he could approach the game without having to plan his shots or his strategy. He can come in, look at the situation, and pick out his shots immediately. He knows how they'll connect and how they'll cut together, so he cuts as he goes along. It's amazing. I've never seen anyone work that fast. Also, he's confident enough with himself to put the priority on the work. If an actor, or anybody else involved in the production, has an idea or a concept, he's completely receptive, which makes all the actors real comfortable.

—Vin Diesel, actor

Left: (Left to right) Tom Hanks,
Steven Spielberg, Ed Burns.
Top: Steven Spielberg, Matt Damon
Right: Jeremy Davies

"The real stars on the beach were the members of the Irish army who helped us re-create the largest manned invasion in history."
-- Steven Spielberg

Right: Members of the Irish army in full regalia on the first day of filming on the beach in Ireland.

"Omaha Beach was a nightmare. Even now
it brings pain to recall what happened
there on June 6, 1944. I have returned
many times to honor the valiant men
who died on that beach. They should
never be forgotten. Nor should those
who lived to carry the day by the
slimmest of margins. Every man who
set foot on Omaha Beach that
day was a hero."
--General Omar Bradley, 1974

DREAMWORKS PICTURES *and* PARAMOUNT PICTURES
present

An AMBLIN ENTERTAINMENT *Production*

In association with MUTUAL FILM COMPANY

saving private ryan

Directed by STEVEN SPIELBERG

Written by ROBERT RODAT

Produced by STEVEN SPIELBERG & IAN BRYCE

Produced by MARK GORDON & GARY LEVINSOHN

Director of Photography JANUSZ KAMINSKI, A.S.C.

Production Designer TOM SANDERS

Film Editor MICHAEL KAHN, A.C.E.

Music by JOHN WILLIAMS

Costume Designer JOANNA JOHNSTON

Co-Producers BONNIE CURTIS
& ALLISON LYON SEGAN

Casting by DENISE CHAMIAN, C.S.A.

Captain Miller
TOM HANKS

Sergeant Horvath
TOM SIZEMORE

Private Reiben
EDWARD BURNS

Private Jackson
BARRY PEPPER

Private Mellish
ADAM GOLDBERG

Private Caparzo
VIN DIESEL

T/4 Medic Wade
GIOVANNI RIBISI

Corporal Upham
JEREMY DAVIES

Private Ryan
MATT DAMON

Associate Producer/	
Production Manager	MARK HUFFAM
First Assistant Director	SERGIO MIMICA-GEZZAN
Second Assistant Director	ADAM GOODMAN
Associate Producer	KEVIN DE LA NOY
Sound Designer	GARY RYDSTROM
Special Effects Supervisor	NEIL CORBOULD
Special Effects Floor Supervisor	CLIVE BEARD
Stunt Coordinator	SIMON CRANE
Supervising Art Director	DANIEL T. DORRANCE
Set Decorator	LISA DEAN KAVANAUGH
Senior Military Advisor	CAPT. DALE DYE, USMC (ret)
U.K. Casting by	PRISCILLA JOHN

THE CAST

Captain Miller	TOM HANKS
Sergeant Horvath	TOM SIZEMORE
Private Reiben	EDWARD BURNS
Private Jackson	BARRY PEPPER
Private Mellish	ADAM GOLDBERG
Private Caparzo	VIN DIESEL
T/4 Medic Wade	GIOVANNI RIBISI
Corporal Upham	JEREMY DAVIES
Private Ryan	MATT DAMON
Captain Hamill	TED DANSON
Sergeant Hill	PAUL GIAMATTI
Lieutenant Colonel Anderson	DENNIS FARINA
Steamboat Willie	JOERG STADLER
Corporal Henderson	MAXIMILIAN MARTINI
Toynbe	DYLAN BRUNO
Weller	DANIEL CERQUEIRA
Parker	DEMETRI GORITSAS
Trask	IAN PORTER
Rice	GARY SEFTON
Garrity	JULIAN SPENCER
Wilson	STEVE GRIFFIN
Lyle	WILLIAM MARSH
Fallon	MARC CASS
Major Hoess	MARKUS NAPIER
Ramelle Paratroopers	NEIL FINNIGHAN
	PETER MILES
Field HQ Major	PAUL GARCIA
Field HQ Aide	SEAMUS McQUADE
Coxswain	RONALD LONGRIDGE
Delancey	ADAM SHAW
Lieutenant Briggs	ROLF SAXON
Radioman	COREY JOHNSON
Soldiers on the Beach	
LOCLANN AIKEN	JOHN BARNETT
MacLEAN BURKE	VICTOR BURKE
AIDEN CONDRON	PASCHAL FRIEL
SHANE HAGAN	PAUL HICKEY
SHANE JOHNSON	LAIRD MacINTOSH
BRIAN MAYNARD	MARTIN McDOUGALL
MARK PHILLIPS	LEE ROSEN
ANDREW SCOTT	MATTHEW SHARP
VINCENT WALSH	GRAHAME WOOD
Corporal	JOHN SHARIAN
Boyle	GLENN WRAGE
Senior Medical Officer	CROFTON HARDESTER
Czech Wermacht Soldier	MARTIN HUB
Goldman	RAPH TAYLOR
Private Boyd	NIGEL WHITMEY
Private Hastings	SAM ELLIS
German #1	ERICH REDMAN
German #2	TILO KEINER
German #3/	
Voice on Bullhorn	STEPHAN GROTHGAR
Jean	STEPHAN CORNICARD
Jean's Wife	MICHELLE EVANS
Jean's Son	MARTIN BEATON
Jean's Daughter	ANNA MAGUIRE
Minnesota Ryan	NATHAN FILLION
Lieutenant DeWindt	LELAND ORSER

Paratrooper Lieutenant	MICHAEL MANTAS
Paratrooper Oliver	DAVID VEGH
Paratrooper Michaelson	RYAN HURST
Paratrooper Joe	NICK BROOKS
Paratrooper #1	SAM SCUDDER
Old French Man	JOHN WALTERS
Old French Woman	DOROTHY GRUMBAR
MP Lieutenant	JAMES INNES-SMITH
General Marshall	HARVE PRESNELL
War Department Colonels	DALE DYE
	BRYAN CRANSTON
War Department Captain	DAVID WOHL
War Department Lieutenant	ERIC LOREN
War Department Clerk	VALERIE COLGAN
Mrs. Margaret Ryan	AMANDA BOXER
Ryan as Old Man	HARRISON YOUNG
Old Mrs. Ryan	KATHLEEN BYRON
Ryan's Son	ROB FREEMAN
Ryan's Grandson	THOMAS GIZBERT
Stunts	
ANDY BENNETT	JINDRICH KLAUS
PAVEL CAJZL	PAVEL KRATKY
MARC CASS	DEREK LEA
STEVE CASWELL	DIMO LIPITKOVSKI
VIKTOR CERVENKA	GUY LIST
STUART CLARK	DAVID LISTVAN
ARIS COMNINOS	TONY LUCKEN
LAURIE CRANE	SEAN McCABE
RAY DE-HAAN	PETER MILES
JIM DOWDALL	JAN HOLICEK
NEIL FINNIGHAN	RAY NICHOLAS
STEVE GRIFFIN	DONAL O'FARRELL
PAUL HEASMAN	JAROSLAV PETERKA
LYNDON STUART HELLEWELL	
GARY POWELL	MARK HENSON
JAROSLAV PSENICKA	PAUL HERBERT
SEON ROGERS	DOMINIC HEWITT
MAC STEINMEIER	JEFF HEWITT-DAVIS
LEOS STRANSKY	JAN HOLICEK
TOM STRUTHERS	MARTIN HUB
PAVEL VOKOUN	DUSAN HYSKA
SHAUN WALLACE	ROB INCH
BILL WESTON	TIDDLER JAMES
MARK HANNA	RAY HANNA

THE CREW

Art Directors	RICKY EYRES
	TOM BROWN
	CHRIS SEAGERS
	ALAN TOMKINS
Standby Art Director	GARY FREEMAN
Assistant Art Director	KEVIN M. KAVANAUGH
Camera Operators	MITCH DUBIN
	CHRIS HAARHOFF
	SEAMUS CORCORAN
First Assistant Camera	STEVEN MEIZLER
	KENNY GROOM
	MARK MILSOME
Second Assistant Camera	TOM JORDAN
	ROBERT PALMER
Clapper/Loader	ROSALYN ELLIS
Camera Trainees	ALAN HALL
	ANGUS MITCHELL
Still Photographer	DAVID JAMES
Sound Mixer	RONALD JUDKINS
Boom Operator	ROBERT JACKSON
Cable Operator	DAVID MOTTA
First Assistant Editors	PATRICK CRANE
	RICHARD BYARD
Assistant Editors	MICHAEL TRENT
	ALEX GARCIA
	SIMON COZENS
	BRADLEY SOUBER
Apprentice Editor	JULIE ZUNDER

Supervising Sound Editor	RICHARD HYMNS
Re-Recording Mixers	GARY RYDSTROM
	GARY SUMMERS
	ANDY NELSON
Video Assist Operator	NOEL DONELLON
Video Assistant	SARAH FRANCIS
Script Supervisor	ANA MARIA QUINTANA
Chief Lighting Technician	DAVID DEVLIN
Rigging Chief Lighting Technician	OSSA MILLS
Best Boys	RICKY PATTENDEN
	RICHARD SEAL
Electricians	
MAREK BOJSZA	NEIL MONROE
ALAN GROSCH	PETER O'TOOLE
DARREN GROSCH	STEVE PATTENDEN
PAUL KEMP	TERRY TOWNSEND
Key Grips	JAMES KWIATKOWSKI
	JOHN FLEMMING
Best Boy Grip	DEREK RUSSELL
Crane Grip	IAN TOWNSEND
"B" Camera Dolly Grip	DAVID RIST
Armourer	SIMON ATHERTON
Assistant Armourers	DEREK ATHERTON
	TOMMY DUNNE
	KARL SCHMIDT
Property Master	MAXIE McDONALD
Supervising Standby Props	MICKEY PUGH
Standby Props	MICKY WOOLFSON
Chargehand Props	STEPHEN McDONALD
Chargehand Dressing Props	JOHN HOGAN
Property Storage	ROBERT HILL
Props	
JOHN FOX	DAVID ROSSITER
BARRY GATES	CHRISTIAN SHORT
CHRISTIAN McDONALD	BEN WILKINSON
PHILIP MURPHY	
Webbing Supervisor	ANDREW FLETCHER
Webbing Props	STEPHEN BROWN
	ALAN HAUSMANN
Production Buyer	DAVID LUSBY
Assistant Set Dressers	VERONIQUE FLETCHER
	PHILIPPA McLELLAN
Model Maker	KEITH STEPHEN
Illustrators	MATT CODD
	TIM FLATTERY
Art Department	
Coordinator	LAVINIA GLYNN-JONES
Art Department Assistants	JOANNA BRANCH
	PETER JAMES
	ERIC STEWART
Graphic Artist	LAWRENCE O'TOOLE
Draughtsmen	STEPHEN BREAM
	WILLIAM HAWKINS
	PAUL WESTACOTT
Jr. Draughtsmen	ROBERT COWPER
	MARGARET HORSPOOL
Special Effects Workshop	
Supervisor	TREVOR WOOD
Lead Sr. Special Effects Technicians	
DAVID BRIGHTON	KEVIN HERD
PAUL CORBOULD	DAVE HUNTER
JOHN EVANS	
Sr. Special Effects Technicians	
JEFF CLIFFORD	MARK MEDDINGS
IAN CORBOULD	MELVYN PEARSON
TERRY COX	PETER PICKERING
KENNETH HERD	PETER WHITE
RAY LOVELL	
Special Effects Technicians	
MICHAEL BARLETT	JOHN PILGRIM
BRADLEY BARTON	GRAHAM POVEY
DANIEL BENNETT	SIMON QUINN
STEVE BORTHWICK	MELANIE RAYSKI

CAIMIN BOURNE	TONY RICHARDS
CHRISTOPHER BRENNAN	LEE RIDER
ALEX BURDETT	DAVE RODDHAM
PHILIP CLARK	GRANT ROGAN
SIMON COCKREN	KEVIN ROGAN
CLIFF CORBOULD	TIMOTHY STRACEY
MICHAEL CURRAN	PAUL TAYLOR
STUART DIGBY	COLIN UMPELBY
PAUL DIMMER	ANNE MARIE WALTERS
MICHAEL DURKAN	STEVEN WARNER
RAYMOND FERGUSON	DAVID WATKINS
JOHN FONTANA	DAVE WILLIAMS
JOSEPH GEDAY	TREVOR WILLIAMS
ADAM HILLIER	GARETH WINGROVE
ROB MALOS	ALAN YOUNG
DAVE MILLER	

Special Effects Buyer KRISSI WILLIAMSON
Special Effects Coordinator CAROL McAULAY
Special Effects Assistant Buyer KATIE GABRIEL
Prosthetics Supervisor CONOR O'SULLIVAN
Prosthetics Designer STUART SEWELL
Moldmaking Supervisor JOHN SCHOONRAAD
Head Sculptor ANDY HUNT
Prosthetic Crew

MARTHA FEIN	ROBIN SCHOONRAAD
EMMA JACKSON	TRISTAN SCHOONRAAD
BRENDAN LONEGAN	LAURENCE SIMMONS
DAN NIXON	KATRINA STRACHAN
JACKIE NOBLE	GAVIN WATTON

Corpse and Animal
Effects Designers NEILL GORTON
STEVE PAINTER

Corpse and Animal Effects
Coordinator LINDY DIAMOND
Senior Sculptors

STUART BRAY	DUNCAN JARMAN
PAUL CATLING	WALDO MASON
STUART CONRAN	PHILIP MATHEWS
ANDY GARNER	COLIN WARE

Technicians

CATH BLACKETT	WILL PETTY
CHRIS BYRNE	ANDREW PROCTOR
ARON COLLINS	LIZ RAGLAND
LEE CRAIK	GRAHAM ROSS
ANDREW FRANCE	PATRICK RUSHMERE
JOANNE FRYE	JANINE SCHNEIDER
BARRIE GOWER	ROBERT SIMPSON
NINA GRAHAM	ROSIE SHANNON
SAM IVES	ANNABEL TAIT
VERONIQUE KEYS	BILL TURPIN
ROB MAYOR	TANIA WANSTALL
NICOLA O'TOOLE	SIMON WEBBER
SUZI OWEN	JAMES WESTON
ANTHONY PARKER	SHELLI WOODALL
	PAM WISE

Costume Supervisor SALLY TURNER
Assistant Costume Designer DAVID CROSSMAN
Military Costumer PATRICK WHEATLEY
Costume Department Key ANTHONY BLACK
Wardrobe Master DAVE WHITEING
Crowd Wardrobe Master TOM McDONALD
Key Set Costumer MARCUS LOVE-McGUIRK
Set Costumers ADAM ROACH
LAURA MAY
NIGEL BOYD
Costumers RUPERT STEGGLE
PETER EDMONDS
Key Costume Breakdown TIMOTHY SHANAHAN
Costume Breakdown THOMAS LIGHTFOOT
EMMA WALKER
NICOLA RAPLEY
Key Costume Special Effects/
Stunts PHILIP GOLDSWORTHY

Costume Special Effects/
Stunts PETER HORNBUCKLE
Workroom Head DAVID EVANS
Seamstress PAT WILLIAMSON
L.A. Key Costumer DIANA WILSON
Costume Coordinator SARAH HINCH
Costume Production Assistants NATALIE ROGERS
HELEN JEROME
Key Makeup Artist LOIS BURWELL
Key Second Makeup Artist PAULINE HEYS
Mr. Hanks' Makeup Artist DANIEL C. STRIEPEKE
Makeup Artists SIAN GRIGG
CATHERINE HEYS
Trainee Makeup POLLY EARNSHAW
Chief Hairstylist JEANETTE FREEMAN
Hairstylist TAPIO SALMI
Production Controller JIM TURNER
Supervising Production Accountant CAROLYN HALL
Production Accountant GEORGE MARSHALL
Financial Representative JAMES T. LINVILLE
Assistant Production Accountants SOPHIE DASIC
LISA-KIM LING KUAN
Accounting Assistants CLAIRE KENNY
ANDREW PYKE
FRY MARTIN
Post Production Accountant MARIA DeVANE
Production Coordinator LIL HEYMAN
Assistant Production Coordinators TANIA CLARKE
LULU MORGAN
RICK A. OSAKO
Second Second
Assistant Director KAREN RICHARDS
Third Assistant Directors MARTIN KRAUKA
ANDREW WARD
Unit Publicist SUE D'ARCY
Location Managers ALEX GLADSTONE
ROBIN HIGGS
Assistant Location Managers SIMON BURGESS
KATRYNA SAMUT-TAGLIAFERRO
REBECCA JONES
HUGO SMITH-BINGHAM
Assistants to Mr. Spielberg KERI WILSON
MARC FUSCO
Assistants to Mr. Spielberg – L.A. SUSAN RAY
ELIZABETH NYE
Assistant to Mr. Bryce CARLYLE FAIRFAX SMITH
Assistant to Ms. Curtis MARK RUSSELL
Assistant to Mr. Hanks SHARON AIKEN
Production Associate JASON ROBERTS
Production Assistants

JANE BURGESS	GAIL MUNNELLY
CARLOS FIDEL	AINE STACEY

Military Advisor JOHN BARNETT
Casting Assistant – U.K. ORLA PULTON
Casting Assistants – L.A. KARA J. KATSULIS
JEFF McNALLY
Construction Coordinator TERRY APSEY
Assistant Construction Coordinator JOHN NEW
Construction Buyer HILLERY COPE
Supervising Carpenters JOHN McGREGOR
PAUL WILLIAMSON
ANTHONY YOUD
Chargehand Carpenters ALAN BOOTH
FRED MYATT
PHILLIP SMITH
Wood Machinists NORMAN BAKER
WILLIAM SOWER
Storesman LOUIS KING
H.O.D. Plasterer ALLAN CROUCHER
Supervising Plasterers PETER BLACK
MALCOLM MISTER
Chargehand Plasterer KEITH SHANNON
Chargehand Plasterer Labourer DAVID SILVERTON

H.O.D. Painter ADRIAN START
Supervisor Painter BRIAN MORRIS
H.O.D. Stagehand KENNETH STACHINI
Chargehand/Stagehand NIGEL ROSS
H.O.D. Rigger RON NEWVELL
Supervisor Rigger STEVEN POLLECUTT
Chargehand Rigger JOHN NEWVELL
Welder CHRISTOPHER ROSE
Welder Fabricator COLIN GIBBS
Assistant Welder MARK McBARRON
Plant Engineers PAUL MALING
STEVE TAYLOR
Standby Rigger GINGER MacARTHY
Standby Carpenter MICKY LAW
Standby Painter JOE MONKS
Standby Plasterer DEREK SMITH
Standby Stagehand GERRY DELANEY
Transportation Coordinator BRIAN HATHAWAY
Transportation Captain BRIAN BAVERSTOCK
Mr. Spielberg's Driver JOHN COLEMAN
Mr. Hanks' Driver DAVID ROSENBAUM
Mr. Bryce's Driver MIKE FAULKNER
Unit Drivers

GARY BIRMINGHAM	BRUCE NEIGHBOUR
FREDDIE CHIVERTON	SEAN O'CONNOR
KEITH HORSLEY	BILLY TURNER
BARRY LEONTI	

Picture Vehicles by PLUS FILM SERVICES
Picture Vehicle Coordinator STEVE LAMONBY
Mechanics

DAVE FORSTER	MICHAEL TOMBS
ANDY GRAY	PETER TOMBS
JOHN LEHEN	JOHN SYMONDSEN

Catering Services Provided by SET MEALS
Catering Manager DAVID REYNOLDS
Manager SARA CHAPPELL
Head Chefs COLIN ANDERSON
SINJUN SMITH
Chef ED ANDERSON
Assistant Chefs SARAH LINTON
BECKY WISEMAN
Nurse CARRIE JOHNSON
Fire Safety Officer DAVID DEANE
Firemen CHRISTOPHER CULLUM
BOB POLLARD

IRISH UNIT

Production Manager SEAMUS McINERNEY
Camera Operator CIAN DE BUTLEAR
First Assistant Camera CIARAN BARRY
DONAL GILLIGAN
Second Assistant Camera DECLAN KING
DOCHY J. LOWE
Chief Lighting Technician TERRY MULLIGAN
Grip PHILIP MURPHY
Electricians GARRET BALDWIN
PETER O'TOOLE
Props WILLIAM DRAPER
GARY WIFFEN
COS EGAN
Senior Special Effects
Technician GERRY JOHNSTON
Special Effects Technicians MICHAEL KEARNS
KEVIN NOLAN
ANDREW NOLAN
Marine Coordinator ROBIN DAVIES
Marine Safety ALISTER RUMBALL
Marine Riggers DAN BRITTON
ROGER McGOWAN
Shipwright PAUL TINGEY
Marine Engineers DAVE LESHONE
GEOFF RALEIGH
Landing Craft Coordinator KEN MURGATROYD

Landing Craft Crew
ALAN ARMSBY — JOHN MURPHY
RUPERT BARNES — NOEL MURPHY
COLIN BATES — DAVID NEED
ROBERT BRIAN — MICHAEL O'LEARY
STEPHEN DAWSON — STEVE RICHARDS
PATRICK DEVEREUX — GARY ROWE
ROBERT FOLEY — MICK SELLEN
DONALD HIND — STEVE SWEET
JOHN GEAR — MICK THOMAS
DAVID KELLY — RAY TOVEY
JAMES KINSELLA — GERALD WADE
RONNIE LONGRIDGE — BRIAN WALKER
DAVID McDOWALL — SEAMUS WALSH
JASON MOONEY — STUART WESTON
LINDSAY MOORE — DAVID WINN
PETER MOORE

Costume Supervisor — SHEILA FAHEY
Costume Assistants
FIONA BELTON — OONA McFARLAND
MAEVE HUNTER — ANN O'HALLORAN
COLETTE JACKSON — ANN REGAN
LOUISE KEATING
Makeup Artists — JENNIFER HEGARTY
AILBHE LE MASS
Hairstylist — MARTINA McCARTHY
Assistant Hairstylist — HUGH McALLISTER
Second Assistant Director — CATHERINE DUNNE
Third Assistant Directors — DAISY CUMMINS
BARBARA MULCAHY
HANNAH QUINN
Location Manager — MELANIE GORE GRIMES
Assistant Location Managers — JAMES CLONEY
DAVID MORRIS
Production Accountant — DAVID MURPHY
Assistant Production
Accountants — ANN-MARIE FITZGERALD
SIOBHAN SWEENEY
Production Coordinator — ELAINE BURT
Asst. Production Coordinator — CLODAGH BOWERS
Sign Writer — LAURENCE O'TOOLE
Construction Managers — MICHAEL DEEGAN
DAVID LOWERY
Production Office Assistants
MAEVE BUTLER — DICKON LEVINGE
AILEEN CURTIN — KATHLEEN LUCKING
LISA DRAYNE
Nurse — SIOBHAN GRANT
Post Production Executive — MARTIN COHEN
Post Production Supervisor — ERICA FRAUMAN
Post Production Coordinator — SVEN E. FAHLGREN
Post Production Sound
Services Provided by — SKYWALKER SOUND
a division of Lucas Digital Limited, Marin County, CA
Effects Editors
ETHAN VAN DER RYN — TERESA ECKTON
FRANK EULNER — KAREN WILSON
LARRY OATFIELD
Dialogue Editors — GWENDOLYN YATES WHITTLE
SARA BOLDER
EWA SZTOMPKE OATFIELD
Foley Editors — SANDINA BAILO LAPE
BRUCE LACEY
Assistant Sound Designer — SHANNON MILLS
Supervising Sound Assistants — LISA CHINO
ANDRÉ FENLEY
Assistant Effects Editors — DAN ENGSTROM
LARRY HOKI
Assistant Dialogue Editor — MARY WORKS
Assistant Foley Editor — SUSAN POPOVIC
Sound Intern — GERARD ROCHE
Machine Room Supervisor — RONALD G. ROUMAS
Mix Technician — TONY SERENO

Machine Room Operator — CHRISTOPHER BARRICK
Sound Transfer Supervisor — MARNI L. HAMMETT
Digital Transfer — JONATHAN GREBER
DEE SELBY
Video Services — CHRISTIAN VON BURKLEO
JOHN TORRIJOS
ADR Supervisor — LARRY SINGER
ADR Editors — DENISE WHITING
THOMAS WHITING
ADR Assistant — STEPHANIE D. KRIVACEK
ADR Mixer — DEAN DRABIN
ADR Recordist — CARY STRATTON
Foley Artists — DENNIE THORPE
JANA VANCE
Foley Mixer — TONY ECKERT
Foley Recordist — FRANK MEREL
Re-Recordists — RUDI PI
MATT COLLERAN
Engineer — TOM LALLEY
ADR Group Coordinator — MICKIE McGOWAN
Additional Re-Recording Services — TODD-AO
STUDIOS WEST
Music Editor — KEN WANNBERG
Assistant Music Editor — KELLY MAHAN JARAMILLO
Post Production Associate — MIKE CUEVAS
Orchestrations — JOHN NEUFELD
Score performed by members of the Boston Symphony
Orchestra and by the Tanglewood Festival Chorus
Orchestral Personnel Manager — LYNN G. LARSEN
Horn Solos — GUS SEBRING
Trumpet Solos — TIM MORRISON — THOMAS ROLFS
Recorded and Mixed by — SHAWN MURPHY
Score Recorded at — SYMPHONY HALL, BOSTON
Scoring Consultant — SANDY DeCRESCENT
Music Preparation — JO ANN KANE MUSIC SERVICE
Executive in Charge of Music — TODD HOMME
Special Visual
Effects by — INDUSTRIAL LIGHT & MAGIC
A division of Lucas Digital Limited, Marin County, CA
Visual Effects Supervisor — STEFEN FANGMEIER
Visual Effects Co-Supervisor — ROGER GUYETT
Visual Effects Producer — KIM BROMLEY
Associate Visual Effects Producer — HEATHER SMITH
Visual Effects Art Director — ALEXANDER LAURANT
Color Timing Supervisor — KENNETH SMITH
CG Sequence Supervisor — GREGOR LAKNER
Sabre Supervisor — PABLO HELMAN
CG Artists
KATHLEEN BEELER — TERRY CHOSTNER
GONZALO ESCUDERO — BRIDGET GOODMAN
JOANNE HAFNER — MARY McCULLOCH
JENNIFER McKNEW — CHRISTA STARR
PAUL THEREN
Sabre Artists — CAITLIN CONTENT
CHAD TAYLOR
Digital Matte Artist — MATTHEW HENDERSHOT
Visual Effects Production Coordinator — LORI ARNOLD
Visual Effects Editor — BILL KIMBERLIN
Scanning Supervisor — JOSHUA PINES
Visual Effects Camera
Operator — MARTIN ROSENBERG
Visual Effects Camera Assistant — ROBERT HILL
Lead Effects Technician — GEOFF HERON
Effects Technician — DAN NELSON
Stage Technicians — CARL ASSMUS
BERNY DEMOLSKI
ROBERT DOHERTY
Film Scanning Operator — GEORGE GAMBETTA
Negative Line-up — TIM GEIDEMAN
Plate Restoration — TRANG BACH
Digital Production
KATHLEEN DAVIDSON — JENNIFER GONZALEZ
GARRICK MEEKER — ERIN WEST

Digital Technologies — DANNY LEE
JEFFREY YOST
Visual Effects Production
Assistant — AMANDA MONTGOMERY
Color Timer — DALE GRAHN
Negative Cutter — GARY BURRITT
Titles & Opticals — PACIFIC TITLE/MIRAGE

SONGS
"Solitude" Written by Duke Ellington, Irving Mills &
Eddie DeLange

"Tu Es Partout" Written by Edith Piaf &
Marguerite Monnot
"C'était Une Histoire
D'Amour" Written by Henri Contet & Jean Jal
Performed by Edith Piaf
Courtesy of Mercury Records, France
By arrangement with PolyGram Film & TV Music

Soundtrack Available on
DREAMWORKS RECORDS

Produced with the support of investment incentives
for the Irish film industry provided by the
government of Ireland.

THE PRODUCERS WISH TO THANK
THE FOLLOWING:
The British Film Commission
Welwyn Hatfield District Council
St. Albans District Council
The Residents of Welwyn & Hatfield
Herts Film Link
Arlington Property Developments
Irish Department of Arts, Culture and the Gaeltacht
Irish Department of Defense and Defense Forces
Irish Department of the Marine
The Cloney Family
Wexford County Council
The Residents of the City and
County of Wexford, Ireland
St. Peters College, Wexford
The U.S. Department of Defense
The American Battle Monuments Commission
20-20 Extras Casting
Fruit of the Loom
Range Rover
Mar-Key Marquees
Lee Lighting

Filmed on location in England, Ireland and France

Edited on the Moviola™

ACKNOWLEDGEMENTS
The publisher and editors wish to thank the
following for their special contributions to this book:
Stephen E. Ambrose, Sharon Black, Sheila Clarke,
Bonnie Curtis, Laura Fox, Brad Globe, Tom Hanks,
David James, Suzanne Jurva, Jane LeGate, Marvin Levy,
Anne McGrath, Randy Nellis, Boyd Peterson,
Terry Press, Robert Rodat, Mark Russell,
Heidi Schaeffer, Jerry Schmitz, Steven Spielberg,
Michael Vollman, Hurley West,
and Stephanie Wheeler.

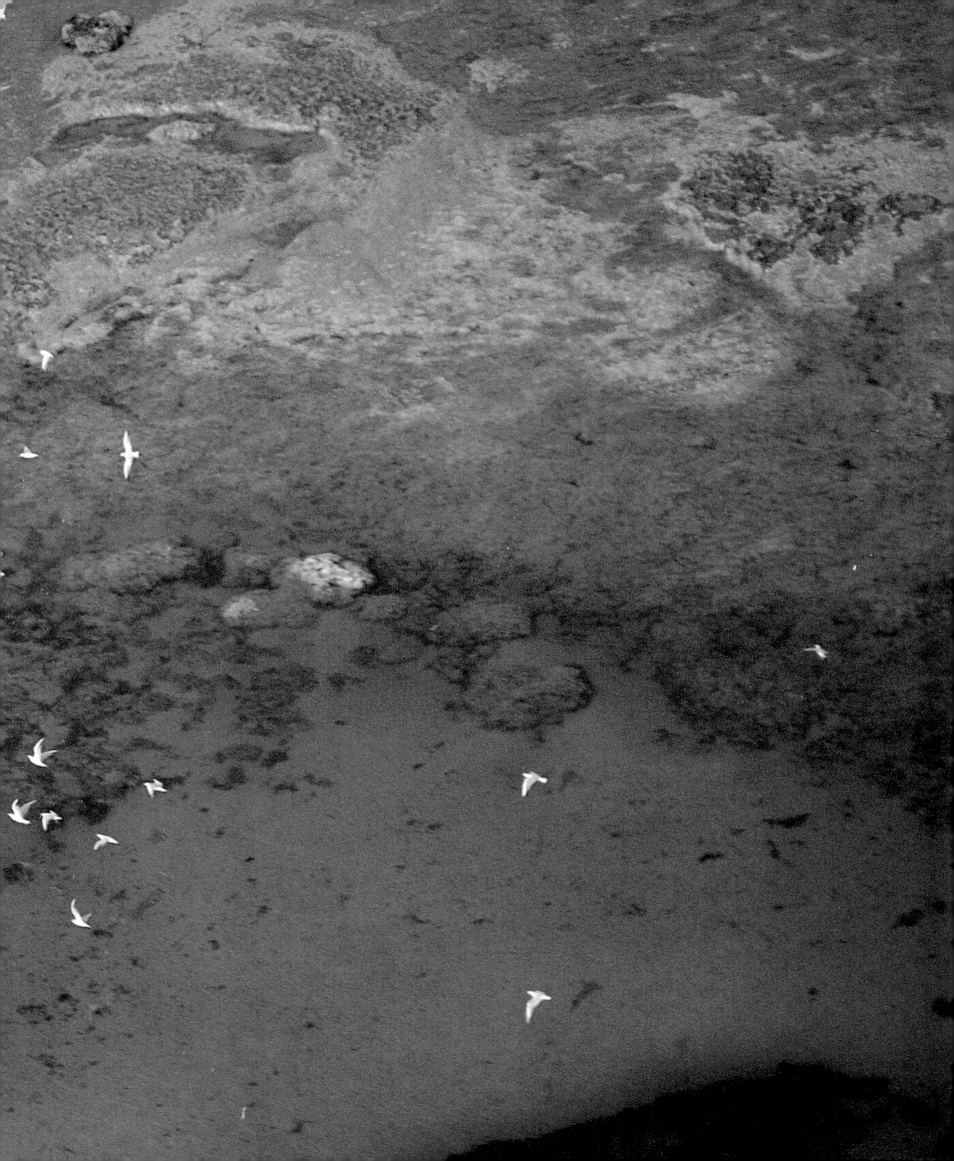

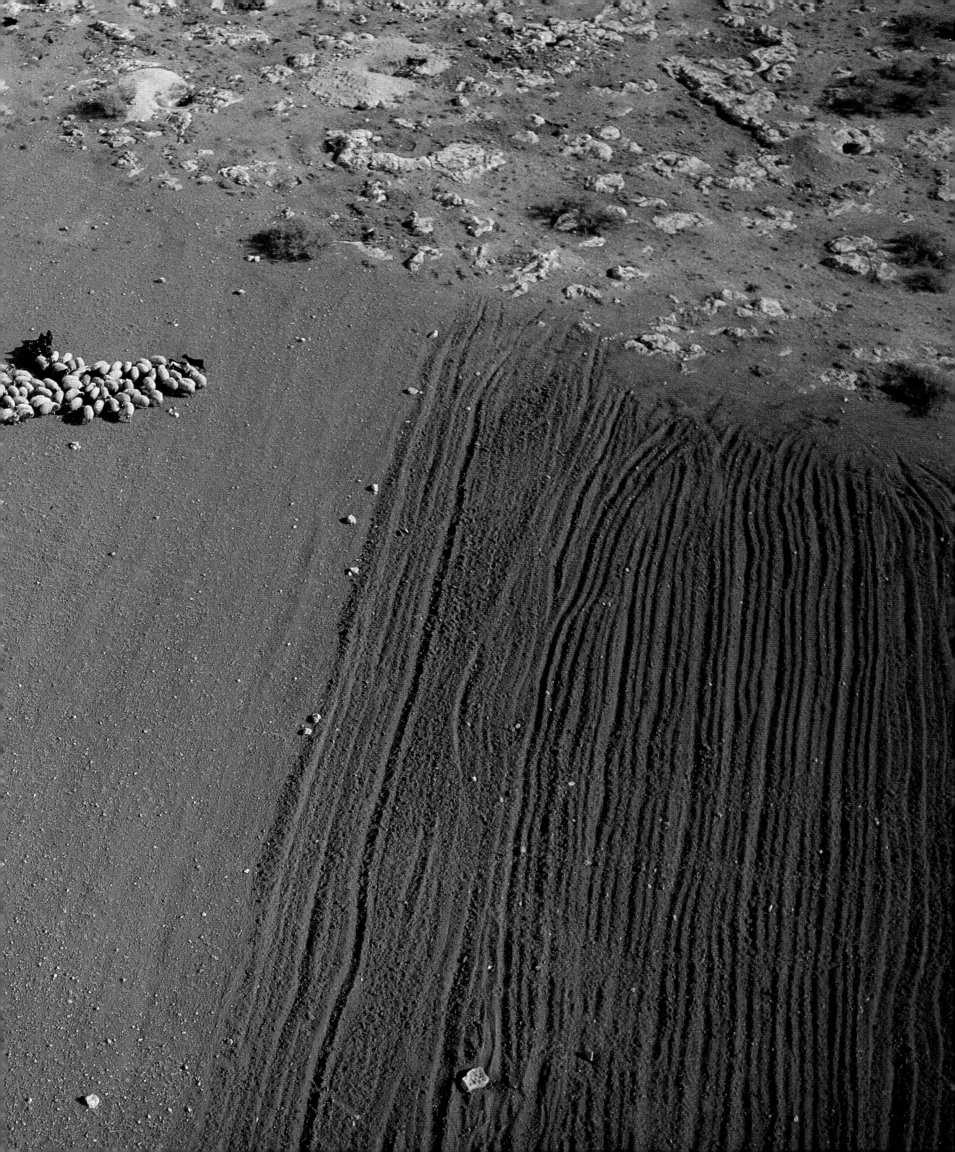

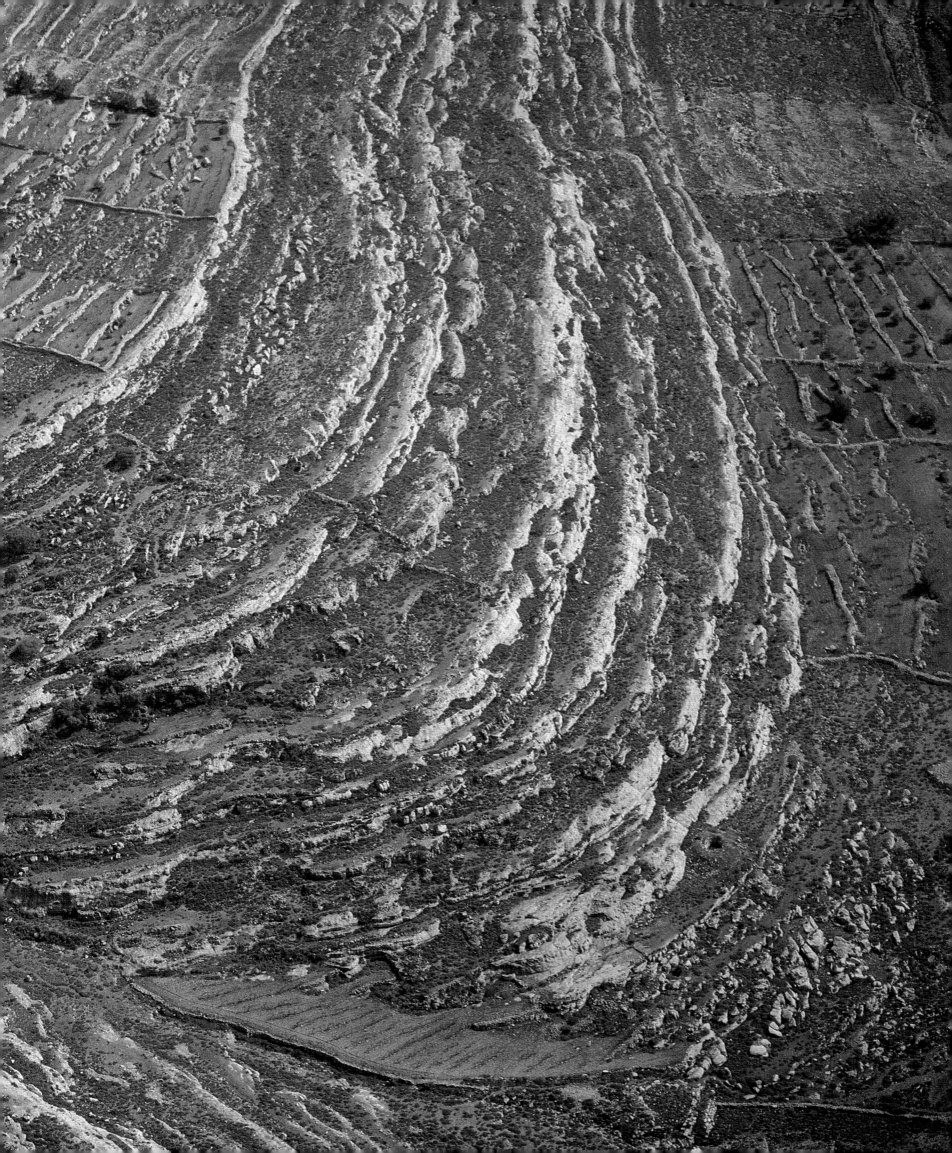

The Holy Land from the Air

Text by Amos Elon

Photographs by Richard Nowitz

Abradale Press

Harry N. Abrams, Inc., Publishers

in association with The Domino Press, Jerusalem

Editor: Beverly Fazio
Designer: Michael Hentges

The publishers gratefully acknowledge the contribution of
Delta, distributors of Kodak in Israel

Abradale Press
Harry N. Abrams, Inc.
100 Fifth Avenue
New York, N.Y. 10011
www.abramsbooks.com

PAGE 1: The wilderness of Judea meets the Dead Sea—at more than 1,300 feet below
sea level, the lowest spot on earth—a few miles south of Qumran.

PAGES 2–3: Birds in flight over the Mediterranean Sea, south of Athlit.

PAGES 4–5: Flocks of sheep at Wadi Farah, in the Judean Desert.

PAGES 6–7: In the hills of Samaria, carefully terraced land. Some of the stone walls that
protect the rich, brown soil from erosion date from biblical times.

PAGE 8: At Beth Shearim, near the western corner of the Esdralon Valley, a vast net-
work of catacombs with more than four hundred magnificent, ornate tombs forms a
unique monument to Jewish material culture under Roman and Byzantine rule. Rabi
Judah ha-Nasi, the compiler of the *Mishna*, is among those buried here: "Miracles
were wrought on that day. It was evening and all the towns gathered to mourn him.
Eighteen synagogues praised him and bore him to Beth Shearim" (Ketubot 12:35a).
The entrance to the necropolis is seen at the center of this picture. The necropolis is
today part of a national park.

Contents

Introduction

Between the river Jordan and the eastern shore of the Mediterranean Sea—along some two hundred miles of the latter—there stretches a narrow, relatively small country, very poorly endowed by nature, which yet, as the land of Israel, as the Holy Land, or as Palestine, figures in the consciousness of millions unlike any other place on earth.

The nerves of three great religions quiver in its dry, dusty soil. Human history in this country extends over half a million years and is more complex here than elsewhere. This narrow landbridge between continents has seen more peoples, cultures, faiths, languages—and invading armies—move back and forth across it continually than anywhere on earth.

Too much time has been poured into too narrow a space. The passenger in a low-flying airplane coming in from Europe over the sea, at about 34 40′ E., 32 10′ N., notices at first a dull film of mist rising over the horizon, next a low, almost straight line of yellow-brownish shore, shimmering in the sun. It is not by any means an inviting coast. There are no offshore islands nor any deep estuaries or fully sheltered gulfs. There is barely a break in the long line of foam where land and sea meet. Below there is still the great semicircle of the sea, green when looked at in the morning but mauve or purple in the afternoon, and, with the sun behind you, almost "wine-colored," as was Homer's fabled sea around the isles of Greece.

The plane crosses low, over the white beach. Almost instantly the view of the sea is lost. The light is harsh, and the first houses come into view, with their flat roofs, densely clustered between the dusty trees, the crowded highways, the chimneys, the bare dunes, and the powerlines. Orange groves fan out in broad green patches to the foothills farther east.

The view is barer than an American or European eye might desire, but it is softened by the haze the heat sheds over all. The maritime plain, a narrow strip of greens and browns and yellows, runs north and south between the mountains and the sea. This was once the ancient land of the Philistines and a famous warpath between empires, from Ramses and Nebuchadnezzar to Alexander the Great, Pompey, Titus, Godfrey, Saladin, and Napoleon. Nebuchadnezzar marched his army down the plain toward Jerusalem and Egypt; Napoleon, with his ambition à la Alexander of an empire in the East, marched his army up the same plain from Egypt to his first great defeat in Acre, at the hands of Sir Sidney Smith, of whom he later at St. Helena said bitterly, "That man made me miss my destiny." Monotonously they have all followed the same great highway, picked up the same pestilence in the same marsh, and fought their crucial battles in the same natural theater, the plain's gateway to Damascus at Megiddo, also known as Armageddon. There the greatest battle of all—the Apocalypse, when the Kings of the Earth and of the whole world are to be destroyed—was placed almost routinely by the zealots who imagined it.

More than thirty centuries have left an imprint in this narrow plain. Canaanites and Egyptians have passed through it, as have Assyrians, Philistines, Hittites, Hebrews, Greeks,

Ptolemies, Seleucids and Phoenicians, Romans, Parthians, Persians, Byzantines, Arabs, French, German, and Italian Crusaders, Saracens and Kurds, Mamluks, English colonialists, modern Palestinian Arabs, and Jews. In the eleventh century, when the Crusaders first reached this coast, it was still covered, as it had been since the time of the Hebrew kings, by a great forest of oak trees—Tasso's "enchanted grove." Later the trees disappeared almost entirely and the plain turned into swamp and moor, a silent, mournful expanse ravaged by centuries of warfare, fever, piracy, and neglect. This was how the first modern Jewish settlers found it in the early 1880s. Its ancient towns, which in antiquity had held over a million inhabitants, lay in ruins, buried under the wandering dunes. The dry land was rich enough but given over to weeds. A few years later, in 1905, a twenty-year-old Jewish pioneer named David Ben-Gurion, the future prime minister of Israel, disembarked at Jaffa. At that time Jaffa was a squalid cluster of houses built of mud and porous sandstone, the accumulated debris of innumerable previous civilizations. Ben-Gurion walked through the squalor and the nearby swamp, contracted malaria, hired himself out as a farm worker, and wrote to his father in Czarist-controlled Plonsk, Poland: "Who is to complain, to sigh, to despair? In twenty years our country will be one of the most blooming, most beautiful and happiest; an old-new nation will florish in an ancient-new land."

Today the restored lanes and stairways around the old port of Jaffa constitute a picturesque quarter of Tel Aviv, the modern town that began as a garden suburb of old Jaffa in 1908. The coastal plain is now the most densely populated, the most urbanized and industrialized region of Israel. As the airplane flies east across the plain, directly on the left is the great metropolitan area of Tel Aviv. Here over half of Israel's population of four million live and work. From the air the city is a sea of asphalt roofs, solar heating panels, and television aerials. High-rise buildings sprout in the business center and on the teeming beach. To the north are yellow dunes and orange groves, interspersed by smaller towns and villages, up to the ancient Roman port of Caesarea and the modern city of Haifa. On a clear day you can see almost the entire country from the airplane. You see the Carmel mountain range, which begins seventy miles away and at its northernmost tip touches the sea. Still farther north is the old Crusader port of St. Jean d'Acre. Only a few decades ago five or six rivers—among them the torrent Kishon—still crossed the narrow plain from the mountains to the sea, as in Judges 5:21: "The river of Kishon swept them away, that ancient river, the river of Kishon." Of those only two or three are left nowadays, polluted by industrial wastes or tapped off to serve a new national water grid pumping water from the relatively fertile north and center to the arid south. Looking down and right now, to the south, you see still more modern housing developments, dunes, orange groves, vineyards, and industrial parks. A crowded superhighway runs down toward the Egyptian frontier. The new port city of Ashdod, founded on the dunes in the 1950s, is clearly visible. So, on a clear day, is Ashkelon, another modern city farther south along the seashore, built on the site of an ancient Egyptian citadel of the nineteenth century B.C. The reconquest of Ashkelon, by Rameses II in the thirteenth century B.C., shortly before the exodus of the Hebrews, is recorded on a wall of the temple of Amon at Luxor in upper Egypt ("Canaan pillaged . . . Askelon taken"). The city appears later in David's famous lament for Jonathan: "Tell it not in Gath, publish it not in the streets of Askelon; lest the daughters of the Philistines rejoice" (2 Samuel 1:20). As you fly over Ashkelon, its pretty, whitewashed houses glitter in the sun; so too do those of Ashdod, and also the massive laboratories, office buildings, and dormitories of the nearby Weizmann Institute of Science, all enclosed in a magnificent park. It is always astounding in this dry land, where plants must be carefully tended and artificially irrigated for nine months of the year, to see such large areas of well-tended lawn.

Farther east, toward the mountains, the scenery quickly changes. There are vineyards and orchards and plowed cotton fields. Huge sprinklers turn, irrigating the crops, and dust-croppers fly in low to spray them. Where the cotton fields reach the foothills of Judea the rocks seem at first bare. As the plane flies nearer, you see the thick brush and scrub and almonds and pines and cypress trees that dot the stony, deep brown earth. Between the shoulders of the mountains is the dull green mass of olive groves. It is a parched and broken land of crags and lonely windswept pines and old Arab villages with famous (Hebrew) biblical names etched in concentric circles into stony hilltops. From the airplane the carefully terraced dark brown land resembles seasoned polished wood.

The villages are of a singular beauty. Their little stone houses fit into the dry mountainside like teeth into a jawbone. There is a merciless clarity here in the sunlit mountain air. The clouds hang stagnant in the sky; their shadows crouch below and cast fantastic shapes on the rugged earth. The sky is luminous, except when shaded by winter rains. At night enormous stars hang in the fragrant darkness like great chandeliers.

The ancient Hebrews were a highland people, and it was from these hills, the "high-places of Israel," that they looked down upon the seaborn invaders from the west, the Philistines and the technologically superior Roman armies, just as in our own century the Palestinian Arabs poised upon these same historic hills looked down upon (and opposed with as much zeal and with as little success) the recent return of the Jews. From the mountaintops, toward the plain, there is a good view of the sea. Settling in the Judean hills in the fourth century, Saint Jerome, used to the vast expanses of the Roman Empire, confessed his astonishment at the short distance from Bethlehem to the Mediterranean Sea—a matter of only a few leagues—and ever since, travelers have been struck by, and remarked on, the close proximity of the well-known legendary and historical sites. What a small country this is, you want to exclaim. And yet a certain sense of spaciousness is enhanced by the stupendous contrast of desert with fertility and by the drama of a landscape bordered on the one hand by the inhospitable sea and on the other by the rough wall of mountains. The mountains rise rugged in the east. The mountains for untold millions of believers have been and still are a landscape of the mind as well: the very heart of the Holy Land, even though, as an eighteenth-century English pilgrim wrote, "Terra sancta being the name only, for all holiness is banished therefrom," by its brutal history and its perpetual disorder. Only a few decades ago the hill country still seemed physically unchanged from the days of Gideon, Saul, or David. Here, according to the Bible, Joshua called upon the sun to lengthen the day of battle and Deborah sang her savage song of victory over Sisra. Here the Canaanites offered human sacrifice to Moloch. Through these same hills Jesus walked with his disciples and promised the kingdom of heaven to all who are wretched and poor, and the prophet who was "among the herdsmen of Tekoah" proclaimed his message of universal peace and justice. Here, according to the Bible, Jacob wrestled with the angel and "called the name of the place Peniel [God's countenance]," saying "'for I have seen God face to face'" (Genesis 32:30); and here the young David slew Goliath with his shepherd's sling and a stone. In the Vale of Elah, where, the Bible tells us this last event took place, the huge dish antenna of a satellite tracking station overwhelms the immediate scene, but a few hundred feet up the steep hill the landscape once again looks as it must have in the Bronze Age, three or three and a half thousand years ago. A few ilex trees, the large robust evergreens that gave the place its name (*elah* is Hebrew for ilex tree), are still about. The vale is the gateway from the Philistine plain to the Judean hills, and the shepherd boy from Bethlehem who the Bible says was sent by his father for news of the battle would only have had to run about ten miles from his father's house to the site of his encounter with Goliath.

In another direction, about the same distance away, we reach Sha'ar Hagai (Gate of the Valley), the traditional pilgrim route from the coast to Jerusalem, and the route of many an army as well. Like all other access routes to Jerusalem from the west and the east, it is a narrow mountain pass, the edges steep and often precipitous. The springs lie few and far apart—a land of ambushes and entanglements where everything conspires to give to the few easy means of defense against the many. From the air you look down on extensive afforestation projects of the last fifty years and the broad, six-lane highway that has been cut rather brutally through the limestone rocks. (A mysterious tree disease that felled large tracts of forest in recent years is often ascribed to the road.) The highway climbs from the Emmaus of the Gospels, where the risen Jesus broke bread with the disciples, and up the road to Abu Ghosh, the biblical Beit Ye'arim, where in the nineteenth century a local Bedouin chieftain still levied tolls on all pilgrims to Jerusalem. To Beit Ye'arim, the Bible tells us, the ark of the covenant was brought back by the victorious Hebrews after it was recovered from the Philistines. Here the prophet judge Samuel again urged them to put away the effigies and strange gods and to worship the true god only. The admonition (it was apparently not very much heeded, for the tribes kept their tutelary deities much as Italian peasants hold on to their local Madonnas) is commemorated by the monumental church of Our Lady of the Ark of the Covenant in today's Abu Ghosh. Farther up the mountain on the right lie the ruins of Al Qastal (with a new village at its feet), which took its name from the Castellum that guarded the highway in Roman days; and on the left is the high hill that overlooks Jerusalem from the northwest.

From here, finally, the city can be seen with the naked eye. Here the pilgrims and the generals in command of invading armies have traditionally paused to behold, piously or covetously, the famous city of their quest, dark against the morning sun, with its ramparts, its gilded domes, its palaces and houses of worship. The Crusaders knelt at this observation point and called it Mont Joye. Jewish pilgrims poised here for a first look at the city and traditionally rent their garments in mourning for its ruins. That first view of the city is as stunning today as it must have been when three thousand years ago the first pilgrims arrived to worship at the first great temple of Solomon, on Mount Moriah, an acropolis above the city. On Moriah, Abraham, according to the legend, made ready to sacrifice Isaac, and, a

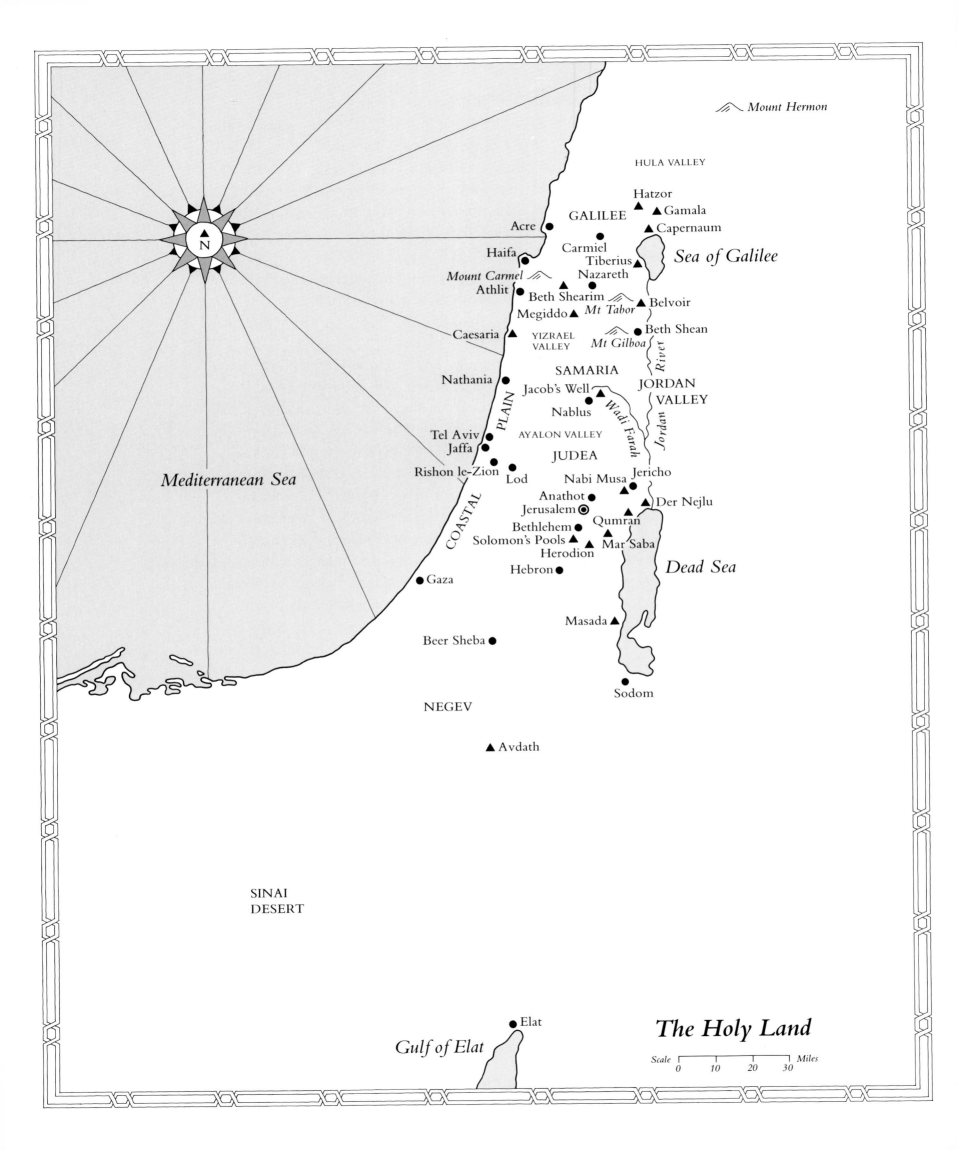

Mount Hermon

HULA VALLEY

Hatzor ▲

GALILEE   ▲ Gamala

Acre ●   ▲ Capernaum

Sea of Galilee

Haifa ●   Carmiel ●

Mount Carmel   Tiberius ●

Athlit ●   Nazareth ●

Beth Shearim ▲   ▲ Belvoir

Megiddo ●   ▲ Mt Tabor

Beth Shean ●

Caesaria ▲   YIZRAEL   Mt Gilboa

VALLEY

SAMARIA   JORDAN

VALLEY

Nathania ●

Jacob's Well

Nablus ●

AYALON VALLEY

Tel Aviv ●

Jaffa ●

JUDEA

Rishon le-Zion ●

Lod ●   Nabi Musa   Jericho ●

Anathot ▲   ▲ Der Nejlu

Jerusalem ◉

Bethlehem ●   Qumran ▲

Solomon's Pools ▲   ▲ Mar Saba

Herodion ●

Dead Sea

Hebron ●

Gaza ●

Masada ▲

Beer Sheba ●

NEGEV

▲ Avdath

SINAI
DESERT

Mediterranean Sea

COASTAL PLAIN

Wadi Farah

Jordan River

Elat ●

Gulf of Elat

The Holy Land

Scale |——————|——————|——————| Miles
      0   10   20   30

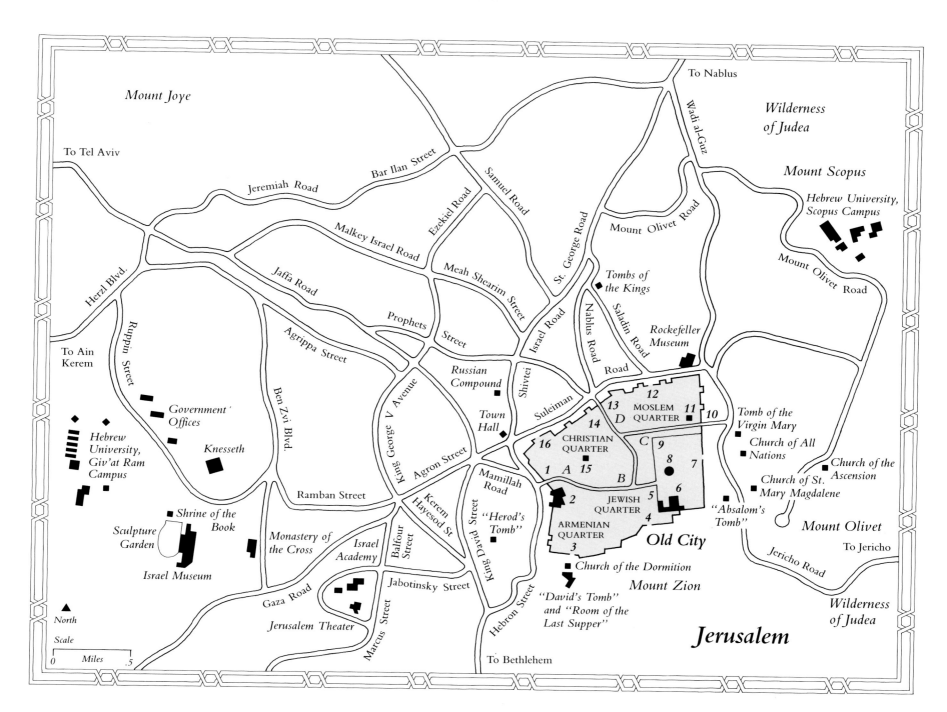

Mount Joye

To Tel Aviv

To Ain Kerem

Jeremiah Road

Bar Ilan Street

Samuel Road

To Nablus

Wadi al-Guz

Wilderness of Judea

Mount Scopus

Hebrew University, Scopus Campus

Malkey Israel Road

Ezekiel Road

Mount Olivet Road

Mount Olivet Road

Herzl Blvd.

Jaffa Road

Meah Shearim Street

St. George Road

Tombs of the Kings

Ruppin Street

Agrippa Street

Prophets Street

Shivtei Israel Road

Nablus Road

Saladin Road

Rockefeller Museum

Ben Zvi Blvd.

Government Offices

King George V Avenue

Russian Compound

Road

Suleiman

13

12

MOSLEM QUARTER

11

10

Tomb of the Virgin Mary

Hebrew University, Giv'at Ram Campus

Knesseth

Town Hall

D

Church of All Nations

Agron Street

14

CHRISTIAN QUARTER

C

9

8

7

Church of the Ascension

Shrine of the Book

Ramban Street

Kerem Hayesod St

Mamillah Road

16

1 A 15

B

Church of St. Mary Magdalene

Sculpture Garden

Monastery of the Cross

Israel Academy

Balfour Street

"Herod's Tomb"

2

JEWISH QUARTER

5

6

"Absalom's Tomb"

Mount Olivet

Israel Museum

King David Street

ARMENIAN QUARTER

4

Old City

To Jericho

Gaza Road

Jabotinsky Street

3

Church of the Dormition

Jericho Road

North

Marcus Street

Hebron Street

"David's Tomb" and "Room of the Last Supper"

Mount Zion

Wilderness of Judea

Scale

Jerusalem Theater

0   Miles   .5

To Bethlehem

Jerusalem

Jerusalem Map Legend

1 Jaffa Gate
2 Citadel of David
3 Zion Gate
4 Dung Gate
5 Western Wall
6 El-Aqsa Mosque

7 Golden Gate
8 Dome of the Rock
9 Antonia Fortress
10 St. Stephen's Gate
11 St. Anne Church
12 Herod's Gate

13 Damascus Gate
14 "Solomon's Quarries"
15 Basilica of the Holy Sepulchre
16 New Gate

A David Street
B Chain Street
C Via Dolorosa
D Al Wad Road

The Holy Land Map Legend

● Cities

▲ Archaeological Sites

⌂ Mountains

millennium after Solomon, Herod built his great temple, which the future Roman emperor Titus would later destroy. Under Hadrian (who destroyed Jerusalem once again and forbade the Jews to approach it) the Romans worshiped a great statue of Jupiter on Moriah, which Constantine, the first Christian emperor, demolished. The Moslems later built on Moriah two magnificent mosques, which the Crusaders turned into churches and the Moslems later converted back into mosques that are still there today, all on the same site. On Moriah the ramparts are all around, and behind Moriah the hilltops of Moab across the Jordan Valley swim in the far distance on pillows of pellucid air. We are at the meeting point of three climatic zones here, the Mediterranean, the central Asian steppe, and the desert, each with its own fauna and flora. As one pauses within sight of the city, stunned, on the edge of the fertile land, facing the stony wilderness and the rising sun, there seems to be no place like Jerusalem on the entire earth. From the air the view is even more breathtaking than from the ground.

It is an impression that no amount of familiarity can blunt. The city hangs on the watershed between the farmed land and the desert, which runs up almost to its gates. The bare, blue-gray hills open to a sudden view of swelling domes and towering minarets. A long line of wall, massive and imposing on its first-century base of colossal stones, is surmounted by a golden dome, superbly built, lustrous with Persian tiles against the translucent sky, a magnificent peacock rising from an immense stone platform. The sky above burns like a heated opal through the air; the walled-in mass of battlements within battlements and domes and churchtowers and minarets resembles nothing less than a ship sailing above the deep ravine into the tawny stone of the nearby wilderness. The very name Zion denotes its being "waterless," "parched," from the Hebrew *ziya*. And beyond the old city, with its ramparts and towers and elaborate gates that fewer than one hundred years ago still opened directly onto the desert mountainside, is the new modern city of close to half a million inhabitants.

Few capitals lie so high, or are so wonderful to look at and at the same time so terrifying. Jerusalem leans against the lunar background of the desert, a dazzling expanse, similar to a vast sea. It is the very epicenter of a turbulent country, where faith and superstition have alternated frequently and belief has too often been distorted into zealous fury and sectarian prejudice and persecution. The contradictions seem embedded in the landscape on both sides of the watershed that runs through the center of Jerusalem—in the sharp contrast between the greenery and forest west of the watershed and the desert east of it toward the Dead Sea. In Hebrew the very name *Yerushalaim* implies a duality, a pair of things, a parity between the desert and the sown, the heavenly and the earthly, between peace and war, goodliness and sin. Here fiction has too often found sites for miracles, and fables have usurped the place of history. Here among the stones the Jews first began to live morally—as the Japanese did literally—in a house of paper, the Bible. Recorded history goes back here for at least three thousand years; archeological remains date back almost that long; and the traveler in Jerusalem often finds himself in the position of the fabled hero who tied his horse to a wayside cross in the snow only to later find it dangling from the spire of what had been a buried church. In Jerusalem, even the nonbeliever must confront and come to terms with the phenomenon of faith and its concomitant sacredness. It is not necessary to believe the myths to be facts: the very existence of a myth is a great fact itself. Here, according to the Bible, David "danced before the Lord with all his might" and carried into the city, behind a curtain, the god whose image nobody had ever seen and most outsiders mocked. Here was waged the first long battle between the graven, sensual gods of the plain and the invisible god of the mountain. It is an austere, forbidding site, chosen with an unerring eye to house the temple of the cruel deity of an eye for an eye and a tooth for a tooth. The hills are massed around it, their names at once cherished and dreadful: Hill of Evil Counsel, Hill of Offense, Mount Zion, and Mount Olivet.

The singular beauty of Jerusalem seems to derive from a rare combination of luminosity and bareness. Everything is open to the sky. Here Isaiah cried in the wilderness. Here Jesus wept and bore the crown of thorns and was crucified with thieves. Here, according to the Koran, Mohammed came on his Night Journey and rode to heaven astride the winged white steed. Here the Crusaders marched, contrite but ankle-deep in blood, up the hill of Calvary—a weird union of the vilest and most tender passions, judged by some as "natural" and by others as "absurd and incredible." Here, for almost two thousand years, the Jews have prayed—from at least the twelfth century, three times daily at the present Western (or Wailing) Wall that they might "Return in mercy to your city Jerusalem and dwell in it as you have promised, rebuild it soon in our own days."

Jerusalem might have remained a small hill town. But she became sacred to three great religions, a city of strife, which continues to our own days: among warring Palestinians and Israelis; rival sects of Christians and of Jews; and the observant and the secular. Few major cities on earth have been so often or so cruelly besieged or so torn apart by internal dissent. Jerusalem has seen at least twenty major sieges and assaults—three of which involved the total destruction of its walls and buildings and a complete break in continuity, its natives sold into slavery or banished for ever—and at least twenty other military occupations that caused the partial destruction and dismantlement of the main edifices. Jerusalem has seen eight abrupt passages from one dominant religion to another. Nevertheless, it is a city of dramatic, almost enforced continuity. Like Cairo and Babylon, it is more than five thousand years old. But unlike in Cairo or Babylon, the principal language spoken today in Jerusalem is essentially the same as that spoken three thousand years ago by David to his men as they prepared to storm a small citadel known as Ir HaJebusi on the steep shelf below the present Temple Mount.

Standing there today at the precipice above the ravine, where, it is said, the Last Judgment will take place, one looks down—or up—on history itself. The Jerusalem name first crops up on a sherd of the third millennium B.C., at Ebla (an excavation in present-day Syria); it reoccurs more than a millennium later on a number of Egyptian clay tablets sent from Jerusalem by Abd Khiba, the city's ruler, to his Egyptian overlord. Abd Khiba invokes no deity; he only protests his undying loyalty to Pharaoh and his perpetual loneliness and fear in these mountains, surrounded by so many enemies. What a strange, prescient prelude to the city's future history! The Bible refers to Salem, the city of *El Elyon*, ("Most High God" and possibly a prototype of Yahweh); the Assyrians speak of Urusalimo, the "habitation of peace," and of the "god Salem," who seems to have been the titular deity here in the days of Abraham. Abraham called the place *Yira* ("vision"?; "dread"?). The Greeks identified it with Homer's Solymi. The Romans, after the destruction of A.D. 120, renamed it Aelia Capitolina. The Jews made Jerusalem the high place of an invisible god, and thus, as Edmund Wilson has written, they gave it to the whole human race.

Today the new city spreads for miles over the hills. But only in the north does the new impose upon the old and touch upon the ancient walls. Otherwise, the old city stands visually apart within its walls. It is surrounded by parks and cemeteries and by the deep ravines of Kidron and of Hinnom. Until the middle of the last century there were few houses outside the gates. The country on three sides reached the town walls. As soon as one emerged from one of the six town gates, which were open only during daylight, one was in the open country. Its bleak, brooding beauty had changed little since biblical times. When Ernest Renan wrote his life of Jesus in 1861, he included this countryside among his authoritative sources as a "fifth" Gospel. (The first four were, or course, Matthew, Mark, Luke, and John.) No one, he wrote, could understand the Bible and the origins of Christianity unless he knew the country. Before he sat down to describe Jesus's entry into Jerusalem, Renan climbed among the debris in the heat and dust to reconstruct in his mind the scene where Jesus told the multitude that "there shall not be left here one stone upon the other." Renan mastered the locale and imbued his account with a new kind of factual authenticity. Archaeologists, geographers, and ethnologists have since added to the record and vastly expanded our understanding of ancient history and geography. Today it is even stranger to reflect, or to wonder as Edmund Wilson did, how from these bare hills and pale contours came the legends that inspired the blazing colors of the Renaissance and the Baroque—that teeming of flesh and gorgeous silks and velvet, the beautiful blond Madonnas, the blue-eyed shepherds, Bathsheba in her bath, Susanah and the Elders in the lush surroundings of near Arcadian bliss, or at least fertility. It is as curious to note that in the Bible itself, the concrete features of this countryside, its cities and villages, are barely recorded except in a most general and abstract sense. Compare its style with that of the almost contemporary *Iliad* and *Odyssey* of Homer, both of which are so rich in vivid descriptions of great accuracy and plasticity. The comparison brings out an important feature of the ancient Hebrew civilization. Homer gives a clear sense of place. He appeals to the eye as well as to the ear. But the Bible appeals to the ear, and its descriptions of places and people are ephemeral. We are told that Jerusalem, or Jacob's wife, Rachel, was beautiful but not why or how. We are not given anything to convey a sense of plan—no shapes, no color or perspective, no interiors, few exteriors, no texture. The Bible tells us nothing of the dramatic, three-dimensional character of Jerusalem, to a modern eye so reminiscent of Toledo in Goya's famous painting. The reason for this absence of visual detail seems clear. The Greeks were a people of the eye and the visual form. The ancient Hebrews were a people of the ear, or, as Martin Buber wrote, they were a people of the *Anruf*. God appeared to them as sound, not as vision. Hence the appeals "Hear O Israel." In an incomparable scene in the Bible (Exodus 20:18), God descended upon Mount Sinai in fire, "and all the people *saw* the *thunderings*" (the Hebrew original says they "saw the *sound*").

When God's angel calls to Abraham—or to some prophet—he is answered "*Hineni*" (behold, here I am), but we rarely know where he is. The Bible has its clear order of priorities. We are given a minute, detailed description of the Ark of the Covenant, but of Jerusalem we are told only that it is "builded as a city that is compact together" (Psalm 122). No story in the Bible is as vivid as David's, at once human and dramatic, and under the stress of great passions: David as a lover, David as a friend, David as a rebel outcast, David listening to the complaints of his soldiers against himself, David tenderly warmed by a young maiden through the cold and feebleness of old age. And yet we never get a visual sense of where all this drama and melodrama are taking place. The prophets too foresee, but do not see: Jeremiah only *hears* across the land the noise of many people at Anathot, one of the most extraordinary landscapes in the Holy Land, a few miles north of Jerusalem overlooking the Dead Sea. Nor are the Gospels any different in this sense, although they were apparently originally written in Greek. Unlike the works of Homer, or any number of later Greek authors might have, they tell us nothing about the shape, or look, or feel of things on the Mount of Olives as Jesus sat there among his disciples, crying "O Jerusalem, Jerusalem, thou that killest the prophets" (Matthew 23:37).

Standing on Mount Olivet today, among the tourists, the vendors of souvenirs and cold drinks, and the camels for hire to mount and be photographed on, you look out on the right to the new campus of the Hebrew University on Mount Scopus. Scopus stands 2,736 feet above sea level. Up there it can be freezing cold in the winter, and the university, with its ultramodern facilities and computers linked by satellite with similar research facilities all over the globe, might be buried under snow.

Then you look down to your left. The road runs down the mountain to Jericho (820 feet below sea level), the lowest and the oldest town on earth, some twenty minutes away. In Jericho it is eternal summer among the palms and the flowering mangoes and flame trees. Tents of the Bedouin, recently come across the river Jordan from the wild Ghor like the Hebrew tribes in the Middle Bronze Age, are pitched alongside an ancient canal. In this country, in one short afternoon, you may have your pick of the climate and the century of your choice.

The road to Jericho passes through the bare, roughly hewn wilderness. The heat soars out of the Jordan Valley far below and singes the skin. Above the vast, desolate expanse of parched, dead soil, the sky rises in a blinding glare. Across the river valley, on the other side, glows the mountain wall of Moab. From Moab, Moses saw the Promised Land but could not enter. Judging from what you see today, it cannot have been a rose garden nor a land of milk and honey. At noon in this weird wasteland between Jerusalem and Jericho, the glare hangs over, and on the burnt-out ground are only blacks and whites—as in the mind of a fanatic, no shadows or muted colors in between. The sheer drop from the top of the mountain to the Dead Sea—the lowest spot on earth—is more than three thousand feet.

There are views here that few countries can match for sheer drama and contrast: the first view of the Dead Sea below, white with vast encrustations of salt, like packed ice in the arctic; the view up from Jericho toward the Jebel Quarantal, with its monastery and little chapels carved into the sharp, steep mountainside on the site traditionally identified as the Mount of Temptation; the mountains of Moab in the afternoon, pink, yellow, and bare. The monastery of St. George clings to the cliff of the Wadi Kelt, and nearby is Mar Saba, both occupied by hermits and monks continuously from the fourth century, when over a hundred such monasteries existed in the area. Only a few miles from Mar Saba are the remains of Qumran—the community center of the Essenes where the Dead Sea scrolls were found— the very first of these great cavernous retreats for men and women who did not flee the world but, believing that they could live here more fully, fervently filled the caves with messianic hopes and speculations. Many were leading scholars and prominent in the affairs of their time. And, south of Qumran, about halfway along the Dead Sea shore, stands the great rock of Masada; like Jerusalem it resembles a magnificent ship sailing on the edge of time into the surrounding wilderness. Masada was the scene of one of the most dramatic events in ancient history, the mass suicide of the Jewish zealots, men, women, and children who had withdrawn here after the fall of Jerusalem to make a last, hopeless stand against the Romans. Masada is probably the most spectacular site of them all.

Jericho, the green oasis at the northern end of the Dead Sea, is as lush and fertile from the air as it is on the ground. An elaborate grid of small, intersecting canals bears witness to its wealth and ample, but carefully regulated water reserves. It is the oldest town of which we know; here man built citadels for war and forged arrowheads of stone even before he domesticated certain animals and plants. Ancient Greeks and Romans spread Jericho's fame as a major producer of dates and balsam. In the Bible Jericho was "the city of palm trees," and of "Rahab the harlot," the city whose walls had come down flat at the sound of Joshua's trumpets. The extravagant claim in the Mishnah that in Jericho one could hear the Levites singing in the temple in Jerusalem emphasized the proximity of the two cities, even at the time when traffic was mostly on foot. Flying over it, you are back up the mountains in a few minutes. The mountain range north of Jerusalem seems forbidding and austere, with patches of light green on the dark brown earth and vistas down the deep valleys that run west from the watershed to the sea and east into the desert. Over Nablus, the ancient Shechem, you reach the famous point from which, on a clear day, the whole land, "from Dan to Beersheba," can be seen through a pair of medium-powered binoculars. The major physical features of the country are clearly visible—the four parallel strips of plain-mountain-desert-plain— as well as most of the famous sites of its history. Toward the north, above the haze, lies the snow-capped summit of Mount Hermon, to the west the sea, to the south the massed mountains sweeping down almost to the Negev Desert, and to the east the great wide gulf of the Jordan Valley that runs from the Lake of Tiberias down to the Dead Sea. Directly below, in Nablus, are the twin mountains of Ebal and Gerizim, and between them the highway by which, says the Bible, the patriarch Abraham first entered Canaan from Ur of the Chaldees. On this highway the famous promise "Unto thy seed will I give this land" was first uttered. The highway is now a main thoroughfare in the Palestinian Arab city of Nablus. The houses of Nablus climb halfway up the hills of Ebal and Gerizim, but their summits remain bare.

Behind Ebal, in the high tableland, lie the remains of a great Roman forum of the Second and Third centuries. The magnificent columns stand on the ruins of Samaria, which, the Bible tells us, was the capital of the kingdom of Israel in the eighth and seventh centuries B.C., before its destruction by the Assyrians. The land is more open here than uphill, and this is, perhaps, the reason why we read of so many chariots in these parts, and rarely if ever in Jerusalem. This is King Ahab's countryside, and that of his wicked queen, Jezebel. The story in I Kings (22:38) of Ahab's gruesome funeral comes to mind: they "washed the chariot in the pool of Samaria; and the dogs licked up his blood."

The farther north you now fly the more pleasant the land becomes. Yizrael (Esdraelon) is the wide valley behind Samaria. Yizrael was the home of the tribe of Issachar; its early fertility is well drawn in the picturesque biblical metaphor:

> Issachar is a strong ass
> couching down between two burdens:
> And he saw that rest was good,
> and the land that it was pleasant (Genesis 49:14–15).

It has been said of Yizrael that for the highlander looking down on it from Samaria it must have seemed an unusually pleasant land with ample room in which to stretch and lie happy. Much of it was swamp or given to weeds when the first Jewish settlers came here early in this century. Nowadays it is full of prosperous kibbutzim. The kibbutzim work the fertile land and grow fish in the large ponds. From the air the ponds are huge mirrors at the foot of Mount Gilboa. On Gilboa, the Bible tells us, the wounded Saul fell on his sword and David cursed the hills in his dirge:

> Ye mountains of Gilboa,
> let there be no dew,
> neither let there be rain upon you,
> nor fields of offerings (2 Samuel 1:21).

Some of them are still bare. On others intensive afforestation has been accomplished in recent years. Gilboa stands like a wall south of the valley of Yizrael. Directly ahead is Mount Tabor, like a huge breast rising out of the plain. And what a plain it is, in the history of warfare as well as of religion! From the days of Thutmose III to those of Napoleon, who routed the Turks at the foot of Tabor shortly before himself being beaten outside of Acre. Tabor as a holy mountain has excited awe and wonder since the dawn of history (the name derives from the Hebrew *tabur,* meaning navel, center, or birthplace of the earth). For the Psalmist, Tabor bore witness to the glory of God; Christian tradition locates there the trans-figuration of Christ: "And [he] was transfigured before them: and his face did shine as the sun, and his raiment was white as the light" (Matthew 17:2).

Behind Tabor lies Nazareth. Again, the farther north you look the greener the country-side appears. This is not because more rain falls in the Galilee, but because the sea breeze wafts in moisture and the dew is more abundant. There is no desert wind, as there is in Jerusalem, to infect the countryside with austerity. This is the rich farmland of Asher—

"Asher his bread shall be fat, and he shall yield royal dainties," as it says in Genesis (49:20). There is a profusion of brush, shrub, and forest, flowers, corn, and oil.

Turning west you look upon the battlefield of Megiddo (Armageddon) where so many empires and faiths contended and so many battles were fought that in Jerusalem "the great mourning in the valley of Megiddo" was proverbial. And in the east, the lovely Sea of Galilee (actually a lake) shimmers in the sun. The lake narrows at its southern end. It lies harp-shaped (hence its Hebrew name Kinneret, *kinor* meaning "harp") below the terraced hills of lower Galilee. The rabbis said, "God created seven seas but the Sea of Kinneret is his delight." The first-century historian Josephus Flavius was equally enthusiastic as he described the shores of the lake, where, he wrote, the soil was so fertile and the climate so well blended that all sorts of fragrant flowers and fruit trees grew in great profusion all year long. The trees today—there are a great many—are mostly of recent origin. Fifty years ago the cliffs surrounding the lake were still arid moor, strewn with huge boulders of lava and pumice stone. When the first Zionist pioneers arrived on the southern shore in 1909, there were no trees except, probably, one lonely palm, of which the poetess Rachel Bluwstein, one of the pioneers, wrote: "By the sea of Galilee, a stunted tattered palm."

Many trees now stand in thickets, and tall cypresses and carobs and oaks line the wide strip of park between the sea and the little white houses along the shore. It is a soft, dreamy landscape, strangely, almost mystically transfigured on a hazy day, a land of utopian dreams, a meeting point of the real and the imagined. In the tranquil atmosphere of the mountain lake, Jesus moved among simple fishermen and preached a gospel of love and of peace; it is difficult to imagine a more fitting setting. Here too, the first kibbutz was established in 1911, intended by its founders to be another Eden, a kingdom of saints in a new world purged of suffering and sin. Its founders lie buried today in a little graveyard by the lake, like a race of seafarers. Their descendants live in neat little houses shaded by huge trees. In the distance you see the modern resort town of Tiberias, and Tabha and Capernaum, where Christ pronounced the Beatitudes. The Jordan River enters the lake through a narrow gorge in the north and exits in the south, shaded by heavy eucalyptus trees. The thick undergrowth covers both banks all along its serpentine course. The Jordan amazes by its narrowness: it is a brook by European or American standards. It does not roll. It trickles. But in the distance the snow-capped summit of Mount Hermon rises majestically above the clouds.

The Holy Land. The Heavenly and the Earthly in a land of dreams, some gorgeous, others perfectly wild. In this book, in Richard Nowitz's wonderful sequence of aerial photographs, we have tried to show a little of both.

OPPOSITE: Old stone quarries in the coastal plain north of Lod, southeast of Tel Aviv.

OVERLEAF: The valley of Ayalon, in the Judean foothills between the coastal plain and the Judean Hills; according to the Bible, Joshua made the moon stand still here and the sun at Gibeon.

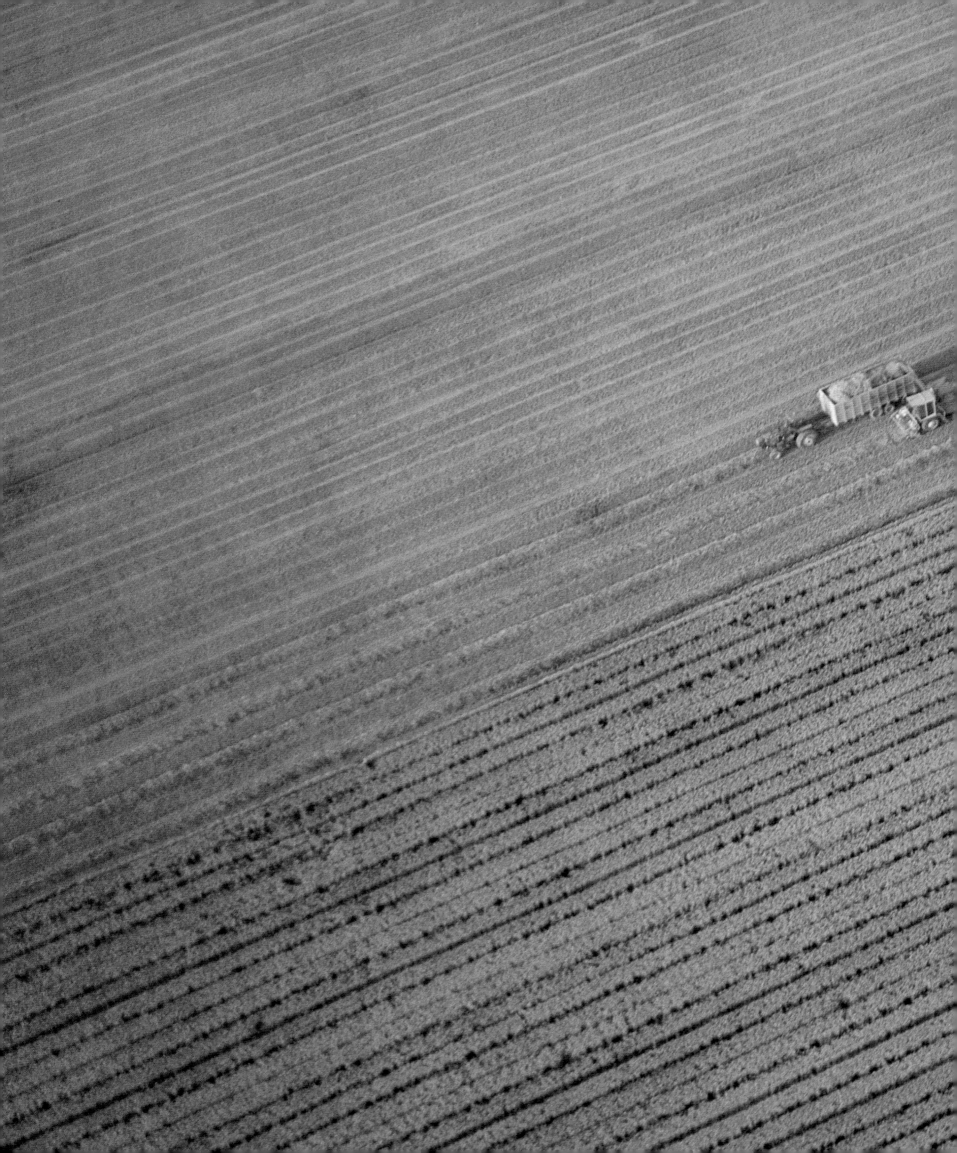

ABOVE: Tel Aviv, the economic and social center of Israel and the first all-Jewish city in modern Israel, was founded in 1908 as a garden suburb of old Jaffa. Literally "Hill of Spring," it may well be the only major city in the world today named after a book—Theodor Herzl's utopian novel of 1903, *Altneuland*, translated into Hebrew as *Tel Aviv* ("Then I came to them of the captivity at Tel-abib"; Ezekiel 3:15).

OPPOSITE: Old Jaffa on the Mediterranean shore. The site is one of the oldest continuously inhabited places in the world. It is mentioned in the list of port cities conquered by Thutmose III in the sixteenth century. To the "haven of Joppa" cedars of Lebanon were sent in floats for the building of successive temples in Jerusalem. Until the 1920s, when the port of Haifa was dug, Jaffa was the main seaport and trading center of the Holy Land and the pilgrims' gate to Jerusalem. Ships moored at some distance from the shore, and passengers were ferried in through a series of protruding rocks to which, according to Greek myth, Andromeda had been chained by the dragon. The first Zionist pioneers came ashore here in 1882. Today Jaffa is a part of the metropolitan area of Tel Aviv. The little port serves only fishing and pleasure boats.

OVERLEAF: One of the two Roman aqueducts at Caesarea built in the time of Herod.

ABOVE: Prehistoric caves near Zichron Yaakov, a wine-making village on the western slope of Mount Carmel.

OPPOSITE: Caesarea, on the Mediterranean coast about halfway between Haifa and Jaffa, was the capital city under Roman and Byzantine rule and later a Crusader fortress. It was renowned in the ancient world for the splendor of its buildings and the spectacles held in its circus and theater, seen here. Inside the theater was found a Latin inscription commemorating Pontius Pilate, "who made and dedicated this Tibereum to the Divine Augustus."

OVERLEAF: An uninviting coast: there is barely a break in the long line where land and sea meet on the Mediterranean south of Tel Aviv. The maritime plain is a narrow strip of greens, browns, and yellows.

ABOVE: Rishon le-Zion ("First to Zion," as in Isaiah 41:27, who "will give to Jerusalem . . . good tidings") was the first modern Jewish colony, founded in 1882 by Zionist settlers escaping anti-Semitic riots in czarist Russia. In the 1930s it was known for its vineyards and citrus groves, most of which have since been uprooted to make room for the modern city that Rishon le-Zion is today.

OPPOSITE: The Mediterranean coast south of Nathania, a large resort city named after the American philanthropist Nathan Straus. There are no offshore islands nor any deep estuaries along this coast.

OVERLEAF: Bahai sanctuary at Haifa, Israel's third largest city, its main port, and a large industrial and cultural center at Mount Carmel.

Acre—the Crusaders' St. Jean d'Acre—is still visually a medieval city. The separate quarters built by the city-states of Pisa, Venice, Amalfi, and Genoa for their merchants and sailors are well preserved to this day. The Great Mosque *(left)* at the entrance of the old city was built in 1781 by the Turks, who eighteen years later, aided by a British fleet at anchor in the harbor, successfully defended Acre against Napoleon and his forces.

OVERLEAF: Athlit, or Château Pelerin, which the Crusaders built in 1218 for the protection of the Christian pilgrims. It projects into the sea between two shallow bays. Excavations have shown that the site was inhabited from remote times, certainly by the Phoenicians in the tenth century B.C.

ABOVE: Nabi Musa, venerated by Muslims as the tomb of Moses, is located in the Judean Desert, just before the descent into the Jordan Valley.

OPPOSITE: In the summer of 1947 a Bedouin shepherd boy pursued a runaway goat along the cliffs of Qumran that rim the northwest coast of the Dead Sea and came upon an unknown cave. He threw a stone into the cave and heard the sound of breaking clay. It was thus that one of the most important archaeological finds of the century came to light—the Dead Sea Scrolls. The cave is in the cliffs behind the excavated ruins, the remains of a community center built by the Essenes, the sect that produced the scrolls. Most of the scrolls themselves are now located in the Israel Museum in Jerusalem; some are at the Shrine of the Book.

OVERLEAF: The wilderness of the Judean Hills between Jerusalem and the Dead Sea.

ABOVE: Monastery of Der Nejlu, now abandoned, on the salt soil of the northern shore of the Dead Sea.

OPPOSITE: Mar Saba, named after St. Sabas (439–532), who built the first monastery in this wild gorge east of Bethlehem in the Judean Desert in 482. It is a remarkable fact that even though by the fifth century Christianity was well established as the official religion of a powerful empire, and its adherents were no longer persecuted but offered security, still hundreds of thousands of Christians apparently left the comforts of home to withdraw to secluded desert spots such as this. The largest Judean Desert monastery for 1,500 years, today Mar Saba is one of the oldest occupied monasteries in the world, peopled by almost a dozen monks of the Greek Orthodox church.

OVERLEAF: Sheep corral in the Judean Desert. Shepherding is one of the few occupations feasible in this dry, inhospitable area.

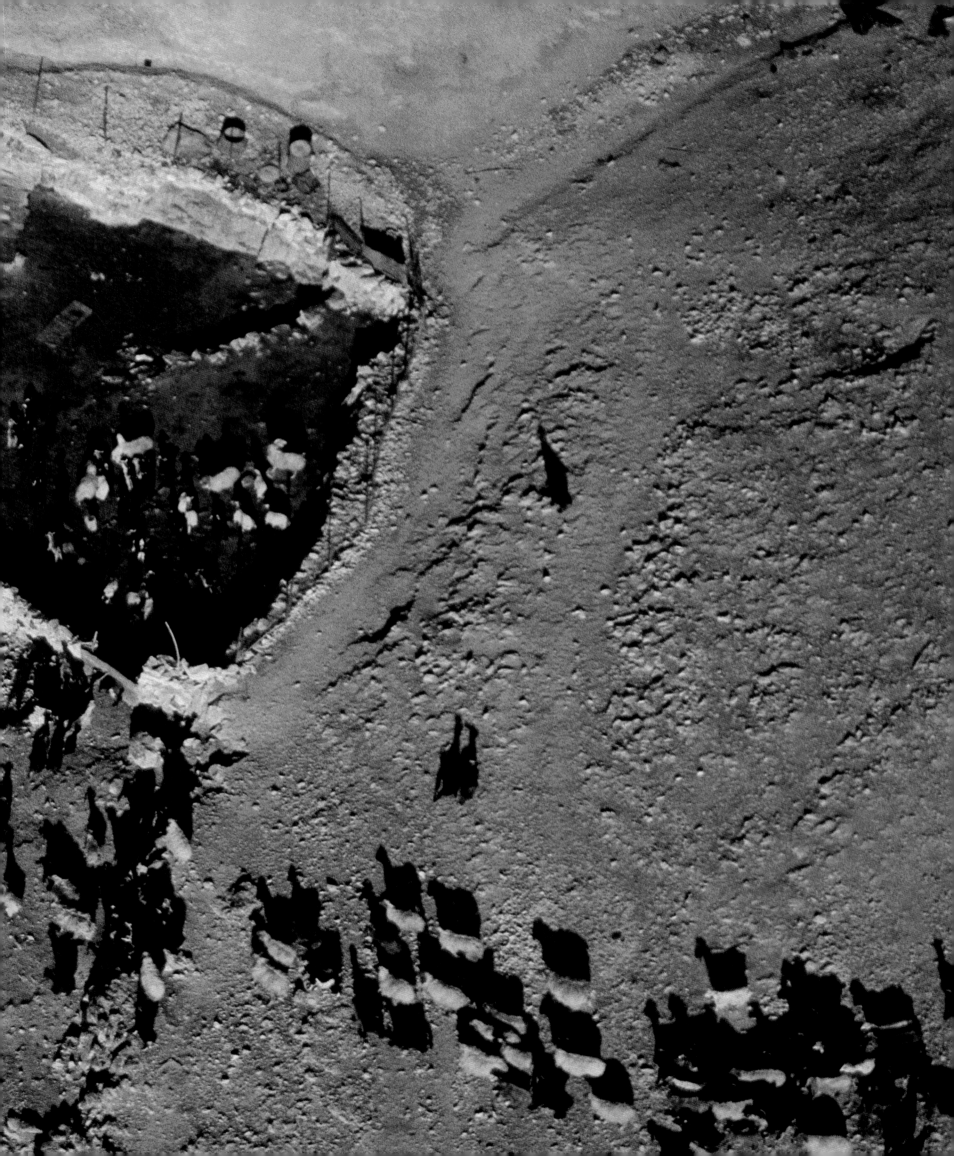

ABOVE: Hebron, 18 miles south of Jerusalem, one of the oldest continuously inhabited cities in the world, is venerated by Jews, Christians, and Moslems as the burial place of the patriarchs Abraham, Isaac, and Jacob and their spouses. The cave of Machpelah is now a mosque (Haram el Khalil) in which, since 1967, Jewish prayer services also take place. The cave is enclosed within a colossal Herodian wall built in superbly cut mammoth stones, similar to the Western Wall in Jerusalem.

LEFT: Herodion, Herod the Great's fortress-palace four miles southeast of Bethlehem on the way to Masada and almost 2,500 feet above sea level, is reminiscent of Roman imperial tombs. Herod commanded to be buried here together with a vast fortune in gold and silver, but so far extensive excavations have found no trace of either his tomb or any treasure.

RIGHT: The Shrine of the Book within the Israel Museum complex in Jerusalem houses the best of the Dead Sea Scrolls and other first and second century manuscripts found in the caves of Qumran in the Judean Desert. Its pointed round roof is intended to represent the cover of one of the clay jars in which the Dead Sea Scrolls were found.

OVERLEAF: The western part of Jerusalem, with the Shrine of the Book, and the Knesseth, Israel's parliament, in the background. In the foreground is the Israel Museum sculpture garden.

· 54 ·

Ain Kerem, the biblical Beth Kerem, in the hills southwest of Jerusalem. Excavations have revealed traces of an inhabited center during the Bronze Age, but Ain Kerem is famous mainly as the traditional birthplace of St. John the Baptist. Its name (meaning Spring or House of the Vineyard) denotes the site's role as a wine-producing area in biblical times. "O ye children of Benjamin, gather yourselves to flee out of the midst of Jerusalem," said Jeremiah (6:1), "and blow the trumpet in Tekoa, and set up a sign of fire at Beth-haccerem." The New Testament does not mention Beth Kerem by name, only reports that Mary had gone in haste into the hill country outside Jerusalem to salute Elizabeth (Luke 1:39).

ABOVE: The twelve cupolas of the Roman Catholic Church of All Nations, at the foot of Mount Olivet, refer to the twelve nations which contributed funds to its construction. At left is the traditional site of the Garden of Gethsemane. A few ancient olive trees still stand there and bear fruit. The garden must have been on or very close to the direct route that in the first century led from the Temple Mount, across the valley, to the summit of Olivet. According to tradition many events related to the life of Jesus took place at this area: hence the many holy sites located here.

OPPOSITE: On the slope of Olivet is the Russian Church of St. Mary Magdalene, built in 1888 by Czar Alexander III in memory of his mother, with its seven characteristic onion-shaped turrets. A flight of ancient steps cut in the rock leads from here to the summit of Olivet.

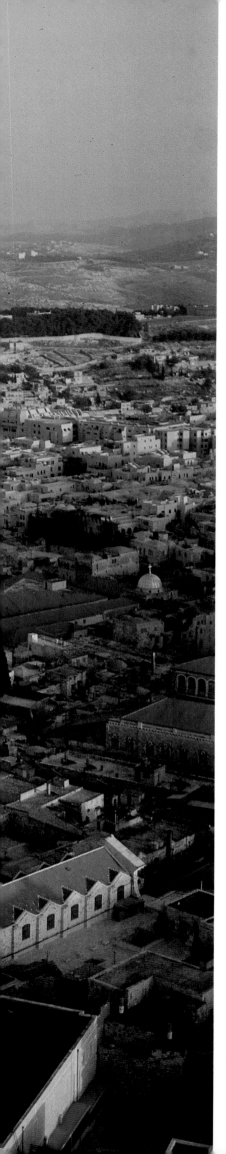

ABOVE: The Basilica of the Holy Sepulchre—the most venerated sanctuary in all Christendom—was built on the site identified since the fourth century with the passion and sepulchre of Christ on Calvary. Today it takes a good deal of imagination to envisage the splendor of the original basilica Constantine the Great built here on the site of a pagan temple in A.D. 325–35; or of that built by the Crusaders, said to have been one of the greatest structures of the twelfth century, a worthwhile companion, it seemed, to the contemporary cathedrals of Chartres and Vézelay. Its outlines can still be determined by the great rectangle formed by the shopfronts and bazaars in the top righthand corner of the picture. In Crusader times the entire rectangle still formed part of the basilica. The present church, a jumble of buildings connected by narrow corridors and chapels belonging to six rival sects, is squeezed in between two mosques and several bazaars. Few discerning visitors or pilgrims from the west have had much good to say about the basilica's present circumstances. It was not only the discovery, which to some had obviously come as a shock, that Christianity here was above all an *Eastern* religion, and that as an *Eastern* religion it had been kept alive during the so-called Dark Ages, but the basilica's aesthetics as well have often been criticized. In this latter aspect, things have changed for the better in recent years: plans for a common restoration of the dilapidated site are finally being implemented by the three main communities—the Latins, the Greeks, and the Armenians.

OPPOSITE: Jerusalem: the city hangs on the watershed between the sown and the desert. It faces the wilderness and the rising sun: a stupendous impression, which no amount of familiarity can blunt. In the east, behind the rooftops and towers, the pink and yellow mountains of Moab, luminous and bare, beckon in the distance. Note the proximity of the main holy sites of three religions: the large dome in the center is the Basilica of the Holy Sepulchre; immediately behind it is the Western Wall; to the left of the Western Wall, the Dome of the Rock on the Temple Mount.

BELOW: The golden dome of the seventh-century Dome of the Rock, designated by Moslem tradition as the spot from which Muhammad ascended to heaven on his night journey, is perhaps the most significant entity in all Jerusalem as well as one of the earliest and best examples of Moslem architecture in the world. Here a Jewish temple stood until A.D. 70, and later, a temple of Jupiter. Under the Crusaders the Dome of the Rock served as a Christian church.

ABOVE: The Jaffa Gate, one of eight gates in the wall of the old city of Jerusalem, stands at the road that leads to Jaffa. To the right, within the so-called Citadel of David, are the remains of three Herodian towers that Titus, when he razed Jerusalem in A.D. 70, left standing as monuments to the valor of his troops. The citadel had in all probability been the palace of Herod the Great: "Adjoining and on the inner side of the towers," wrote Joseph Flavius, the first-century Jewish historian, "was the king's palace, baffling all description" (*Jewish War*, 5:173). Later on, Pontius Pilate, the Roman procurator, has his residence here; here also the trial of Jesus might have taken place. In the background can be seen the Church of the Holy Sepulchre and the Dome of the Rock; behind them, across the valley of Kidron, is Mount Olivet.

LEFT: Temple Mount, or Moriah, where according to legend Abraham made ready to sacrifice Isaac and where Herod built the First and Second Jewish Temples, has been a national and religious focal point of the Jewish people for many generations. At top left is the Dome of the Rock; at lower right is the Western Wall, where for centuries Jews have come to pray and lament the destruction of the temple. The Western Wall originally formed part of the retaining wall built by Herod the Great in 20 B.C. to support the vast platform, still existing today, on which the temple stood. Prior to 1967 the old city houses came to within four meters of the Western Wall; they have since been razed to make place for the present plaza on which tens of thousands of people gather for prayers on the high Jewish holidays.

OVERLEAF: Suleiman the Magnificent, the Ottoman sultan, built the present ramparts in 1540 on the remnants of older Jewish, Roman, Arab, and Crusader walls. Of the six gates he built, all apparently designed by the same hand, the Damascus Gate is the most elaborate and perhaps the finest piece of Ottoman architecture in Jerusalem, as well as the largest of the entrances to the old city. Under the modern bridge leading into Jerusalem appear the excavated ruins of a beautiful, older Roman gate. Behind it, within the city wall, a huge column honoring the Roman emperor Hadrian must have stood (it is clearly marked on a sixth-century mosaic map). In Arabic the gate is still called *Bab el Amud* (Gate of the Column).

Jerusalem, it has often been said, is more thickly populated with the dead than with the living. "Men from all parts of the world come hither to die," Abu Muin Nasir, an Arab writer, wrote in 1047. The city is ringed by a huge necropolis. Its oldest part is in the east, along the valleys of Kedron and Yehoshafath, where according to legend the Last Judgment will take place, and on the slopes of Olivet.

ABOVE, LEFT AND RIGHT: Christian cemeteries behind the Church of the Ascension on the Mount of Olives.

OPPOSITE, ABOVE: For the ancient Hebrews, Olivet was a place of burial as well as of mourning: "And David went up by the ascent of mount Olivet, and wept as he went up, and had his head covered, and he went barefoot: and all the people that was with him covered every man his head, and they went up, weeping as they went up" (2 Samuel 15:30).

OPPOSITE, BELOW: Military cemetery on Mount Herzl, west of Jerusalem, a bitter re-minder of the five wars Israel has fought since its foundation in 1948, and of the many bloody skirmishes in between.

ABOVE: The buttressed walls of the Greek Orthodox Monastery of the Cross rise in the valley bearing the same name, derived from the legend that the tree from which the cross on which Jesus was crucified was made had grown here. The area still abounds in ancient olive trees, which today form part of a large, public park.

OPPOSITE: The Romanesque church of St. Anne, the site, according to Christian tradition, of Mary's birth, is, in its simple strength, a perfect example of twelfth-century Crusader architecture. Next to it on the left are the excavated ruins of the twin pools of Bethesda.

ABOVE: Yemin Moshe, residential quarter, now considered to be an artists' quarter, was one of the first Jewish settlements outside the old city's walls when it was founded in the nineteenth century.

OPPOSITE: Mount Zion on the western hill projecting out beyond the southern wall of the old city. Before the destruction of Jerusalem in A.D. 70 the walls ran farther west and the hill was still enclosed within them. "Zion . . . shall be plowed as a field," it is said in Micah (3:12), "and Jerusalem shall become heaps." The great German Church of the Dormition (center), where Mary fell into eternal sleep, was built at the beginning of this century (1910).

ABOVE: Anathot, the Arab village in the Judean Hills just northeast of Jerusalem, be-
lieved to be the village where the prophet Jeremiah grew up, overlooks the Judean
Desert. Behind the village the land falls away in a maze of broken rocks. The vision of
that wilderness, blazing in the heat, may have been in Jeremiah's mind when he said:
"A dry wind of the high places in the wilderness . . . not to fan, nor to cleanse" (4:11).

OPPOSITE: The campus of Hebrew University, opened in 1925, on Mount Scopus on
the northeast side of Jerusalem.

ABOVE: Bethlehem, about four and one-half miles south of Jerusalem. In the center can be seen the Crusader Church of the Nativity, built over the remains of an earlier Byzantine basilica. "But thou, Bethlehem Ephratah, though thou be little among the thousands of Judah, yet out of thee shall he come forth unto me that is to be ruler in Israel" (Micah 5:2). According to the Old Testament, David, the second Jewish king, was born here. The emperor Constantine built the first basilica over the cave identified two centuries earlier by Justinus Martyr as the birthplace of Jesus. Constantine's mother, Helene, inaugurated the basilica in 339; until shortly before that the cave had been a sanctuary dedicated to the worship of Jupiter and Adonis. There are still today many houses in Bethlehem that are built over or in front of caves.

OPPOSITE: Shepherds Field, outside Bethlehem, identified with the place where Jacob pitched his tents after the death of Rachel and where the angel came upon the shepherds to announce the birth of Christ.

OVERLEAF: "Solomon's Pools," a complex of three large (the lowest is 580 feet long and 50 feet deep) pools that store spring water and catch rain water, south of Bethlehem. For centuries they have formed part of the extensive water supply system for Jerusalem. Elements of the system—aqueducts, reservoirs, and underground pipes—date back to the first century B.C., perhaps even earlier. Today the water from the pools is used only by inhabitants of the immediate vicinity.

ABOVE: Hula Valley, with Mount Hermon snow-covered in the distance. Now one of the most fertile parts of Galilee, Hula was a malaria-infested swamp until the early 1950s, when it was drained.

OPPOSITE: On the Via Maris ("Way of the Sea"), the principal caravan route between north and south and commanding a well-watered pass, Hatzor was a fortress city that made use of its strategic position between weaker neighbors to become "the head of all those kingdoms" (Joshua 11:10). In its heyday, between the seventeenth and eighteenth centuries B.C., the city occupied an area of almost two hundred acres. Archaeological evidence shows that the city was burned down in the second half of the thirteenth century; this has been tied to the account in Joshua 11:13 of the burning of Hatzor by the Israelites under Joshua. Hatzor reappears later in the Bible as a cavalry city built by Solomon.

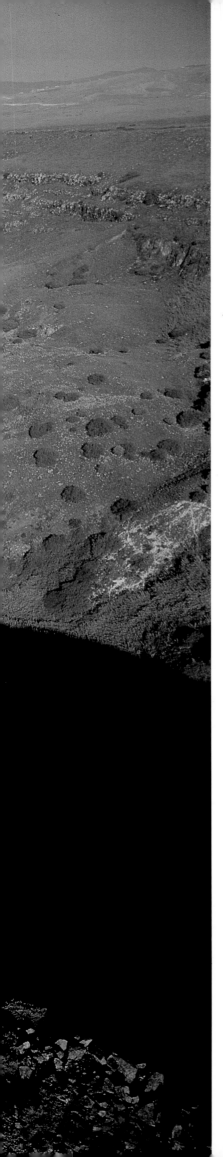

"And the Romans captured all the fortresses (of Galilee) . . . Gamala also which is a city on the other side of the lake . . . revolted against them (relying) on the difficulty of the place which was situated . . . upon a rough ridge of a high mountain, with a kind of neck in the middle . . . like a camel in figure, from whence it is so named" (Josephus Flavius, *Wars of the Jews*, 5:1).

Gamala (*left*) was a natural fortress on the Golan Heights above the Sea of Galilee. The saga of its siege and ultimate battle has been compared to that of Masada. After a long siege the Romans, in A.D. 67, finally scaled its ramparts, and the last of the fighting garrison withdrew to the citadel in the upper part. When they too were surrounded and "despaired of escaping," Josephus reports, they "flung their children and their wives, and themselves also, down the precipices. . . . The Romans slew four thousand, whereas the number that had thrown themselves down was found to be five thousand: nor did anyone escape except two women."

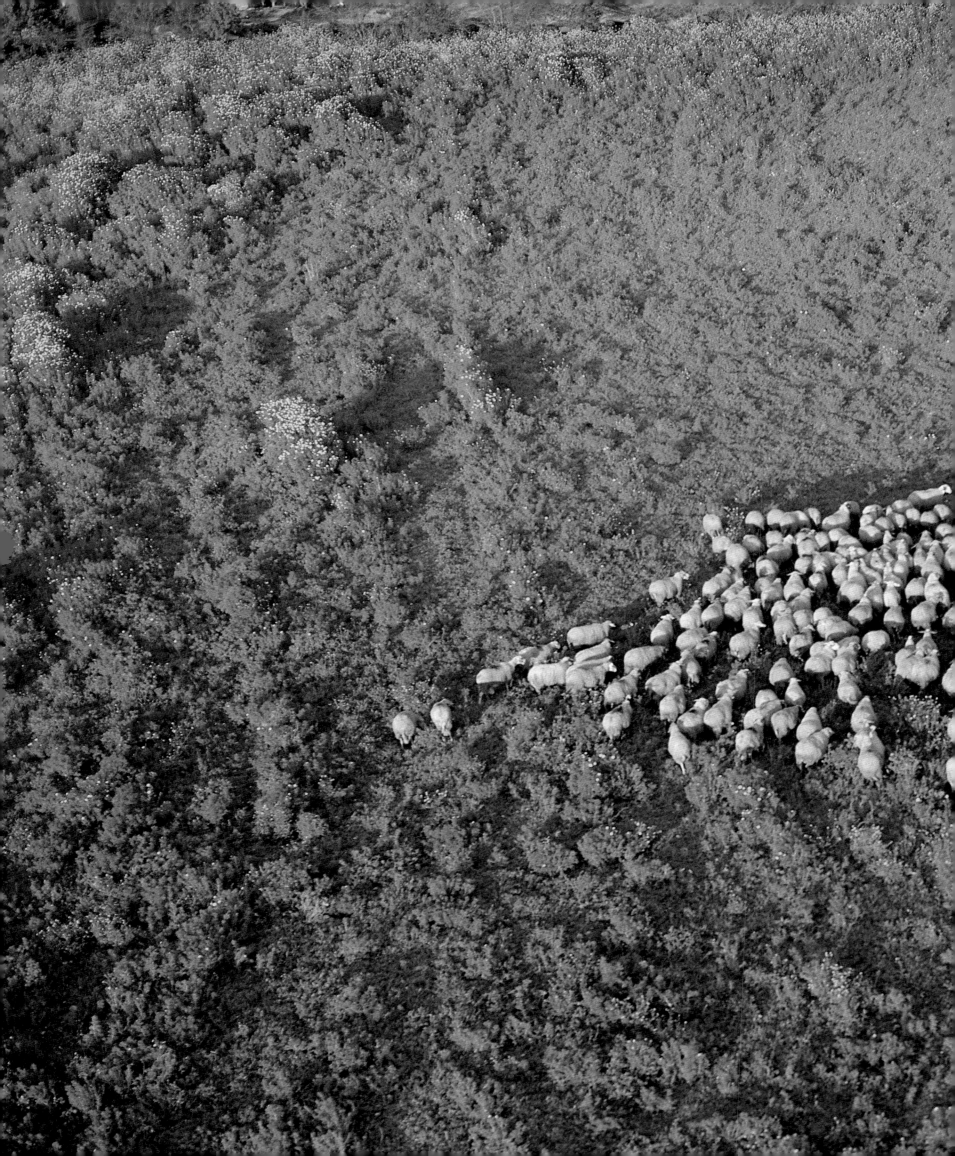

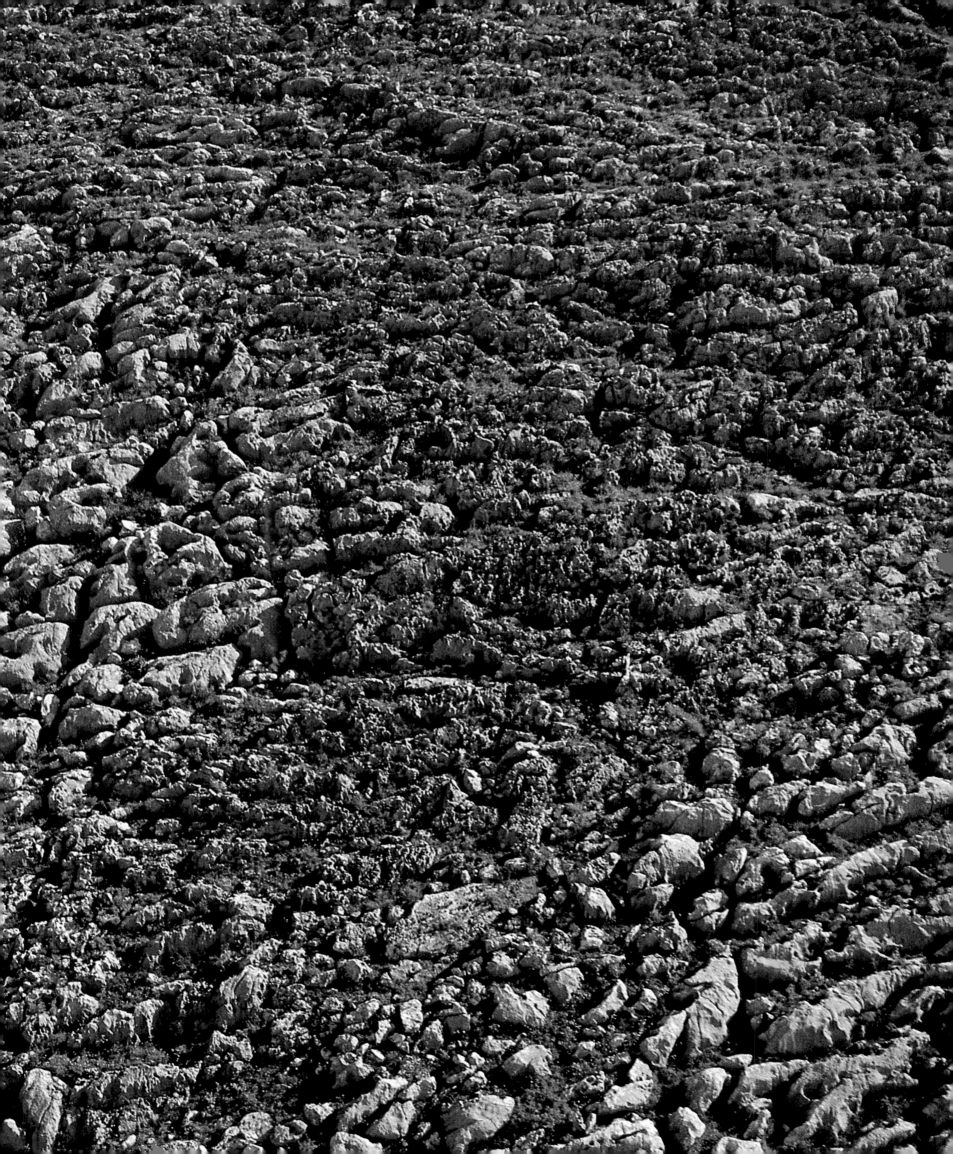

ABOVE AND OPPOSITE: Fields and fishponds, like huge reflecting mirrors, at the foot of the Gilboa mountain range. Some of the hilltops are still as dry and bare as they were in David's lament for Saul and Jonathan: "Ye mountains of Gilboa, let there be no dew, neither let there be rain, upon you, nor fields of offerings: for there the shield of the mighty is vilely cast away, the shield of Saul, as though he had not been anointed with oil" (2 Samuel 1:21).

OVERLEAF: Valley of Yizrael (Esdraelon) near Harod, the well where Gideon stood up to the Midianites (Judges 7:1). There are rich kibbutz lands around it today, and the well area with its natural pool is part of a national park.

ABOVE: The Roman theater at Beth Shean, perhaps the best preserved in the country, testifies to the importance of that city in the first century. The Romans merely continued what had been begun thousands of years before. The natural advantages of the site, on the main west–east highway connecting Egypt and the sea with Mesopotamia, help to explain its long history. Beth Shean has been continuously occupied for more than five thousand years. Its 260-foot-high *tel* (mound) contains eighteen superimposed cities. It was one of the major strongholds from which the Pharaohs, the Philistines, the Hebrews, the Romans, and the Byzantines successively controlled the country.

OVERLEAF: The *moshav* (cooperative settlement) of Nahalal, at the mouth of the valley Yizrael. It was founded in 1921 as part of a great social experiment that continues to this day. Its circular shape was meant to serve (and symbolically reflect) an experiment in rational farming and town planning. The jointly owned services (tractor stations, marketing and purchasing agencies, clinics, schools, etc.) are at the center and are surrounded by a wide circle of equidistant farmhouses and individually owned fields. The *moshav* was a compromise between the collectivist kibbutz and the free enterprise village. It is today the most common form of farming in Israel.

ABOVE: Carmiel, a new city in Galilee founded in 1964 and settled mostly by new immigrants.

RIGHT: The excavations at Megiddo (Armageddon), with the battlefield in the background, reveal one of the great theaters of history, where so much blood was shed in so many battles between so many rival faiths and empires that the name has come to denote destruction in an ultimate, apocalyptic battle. Its position in the plain at the head of an important mountain pass gave it control over the Via Maris, the main highway between Egypt and the north, northeast. Thutmose III carved a graphic record of the battle he fought here in 1468 B.C. on the wall of his temple at Karnak in upper Egypt. Solomon built a palace at Megiddo and stables for his cavalry horses; some of their ruins have been excavated.

ABOVE: Church above the Sea of Galilee on the site where Jesus pronounced the Beatitutes. One is tempted to seek a natural link between a religion of love and this soft, dreamy landscape, as between the harsh and cruel desert land east of Jerusalem and the notion of "an eye for an eye and a tooth for a tooth." Josephus said that the air at the shore of the lake was "so well tempered that it suits the most opposite varieties . . . by a happy rivalry each of the seasons wished to claim this region for her own."

OPPOSITE: Near the church pictured above, the remains of a synagogue have been unearthed at Capernaum.

ABOVE: "We travelled to the city of Nazareth, where many miracles take place," the sixth-century Pilgrim of Piacenza wrote. "In the synagogue at Nazareth there is kept a book in which the Lord wrote his ABC, and in this synagogue is the bench on which he sat with other children." Already a century earlier the church father Epiphanius had complained that in Nazareth no one could build churches because the Jews were still in the majority there, as they apparently were all over the Galilee. Today Nazareth is the largest Arab town in Israel. The cityscape is dominated by the massive basilica of the Annunciation (*bottom left*) on the site where, according to Antonius Placentinus (A.D. 570), a former synagogue had been converted to a church.

OPPOSITE: National water carrier, north of Nazareth. Water is pumped from the sea of Galilee in the north to the Negev in the south.

OVERLEAF: Safad in upper Galilee, one of the fortresses during the revolt against the Romans of A.D. 67–70 listed by Josephus Flavius. After the fall of Jerusalem, Safad became a substantial Jewish religious center, and in the late middle ages the principal settlement in Palestine of Jewish scholars expelled from Spain. The first printing press in Palestine (a Hebrew press) was set up in Safad in 1563.

Summit of Mount Tabor (*above*) with basilica on the site first identified in 216 by Origenes with the transfiguration of Christ (*opposite*). The mountain soars suddenly 1,929 feet above the surrounding plain, and, probably because of its graceful form and picturesque site, it has excited awe and wonder since time immemorial. It has been a sacred mountain at least since the first millennium B.C. Hosea upbraided the Jews for building altars on Tabor to pagan gods. The road winds in hairpin bends up its sides through the striking vegetation of evergreen oaks, lentisks, and carob trees, and from the summit there is a stupendous panorama.

ABOVE: The ancient synagogue at Tiberias, on the shore of the Sea of Galilee. Founded by Herod Antipas (4 B.C.–A.D. 39), the son of Herod the Great, and named after his patron, the emperor Tiberius, the synagogue was an important center of Jewish learning until the fifth century, and again in the middle ages.

RIGHT: Kinereth, the first kibbutz, founded in 1911. The kibbutz was not a premeditated creation by convinced ideologues: the idea developed out of the practical needs of early settlers.

OVERLEAF: Cliffs of Arbel on the western shores of the Sea of Galilee.

ABOVE: Roman theater in Samaria, on the ruins of the eighth-century capital of the (northern) kingdom of Israel. Micah warned, "I shall make Samaria as an heap of the field" (1:6), but Jeremiah said, "Thou shalt yet plant vines upon the mountains of Samaria" (31:5).

OPPOSITE AND OVERLEAF: The Wadi Farah, a perennial stream, runs from the heights of Samaria through arid land down some 3,700 feet to the Jordan valley. Abraham is thought to have come up the Wadi Farah, after crossing the Jordan by a ford, on his way to Shechem (today's Nablus).

ABOVE: Jacob's Well in Nablus, said to be the site where Jacob camped and bought a plot of ground. According to John (4:12), Jacob dug a well here for himself, his children, and his flocks. According to Genesis (33:20), he erected an altar here and named it *El*, God of Israel.

OPPOSITE: On the highway between the twin mountains of Ebal and Gerizim—now the busy main street of the Arab town of Nablus—the famous biblical promise to Abraham, "Unto thy seed will I give this land" (Genesis 12:7), is said to have been given.

OVERLEAF: Samaria is the mountain region on the central plateau of the Holy Land between the Jordan valley in the east and the coastal plain in the west. When the united Hebrew kingdom broke up after the death of Solomon (ca. 930 B.C.), Judea became the southern and Samaria the northern kingdom. The northern kingdom lasted until 722 B.C., when it was vanquished by the Assyrians under Sargon and its population forcibly removed to the east (hence the "Ten Lost Tribes"). It is a prosperous agricultural region, rich in wheat, olives, and fruit, and is today inhabited mostly by Palestinian Arabs.

The Jordan River, the longest river in Israel, below the Sea of Galilee (*above*) and above the sea (*opposite*), feeds the lush, fertile plains of the Jordan valley (*overleaf*).

ABOVE: Belvoir castle was built by the Crusaders in 1168 some 1,640 feet above the Jordan rift valley to defend the eastern approaches to the highlands.

OPPOSITE: Hisham palace at Khirbet al Mafjar, just outside Jericho, an eighth-century Umayyad pleasure spot and royal hunting lodge, included a mosque, baths, colon-naded courts, mosaics, and ornamental pools. Unique among Moslem sites in Palestine in its spectacular extravagance and unorthodox figurative decoration, its construction has been attributed to Walid ibn Yazid, the caliph Hisham's nephew who was banished from court for drinking alcohol and wild living in general, and for preferring the company of actors and singers to that of pious scholars.

OVERLEAF: Another view of the Sea of Galilee. The sea, or lake really, is harp-shaped, hence its Hebrew name Kinneret (kinnor = harp). In the first century, the west side of the lake was lined with Jewish villages. In A.D. 20 Herod Antipas founded the city of Tiberias here. Under the Crusaders the entire area around the lake was taken by Tan-cred, who made himself Prince of Galilee in 1099. On a hill overlooking the lake, a few miles west of here, Saladin won the famous battle of Hittin that destroyed the Latin Kingdom of Jerusalem.

THESE PAGES AND OVERLEAF: The Negev (which means not "south" as in the English translation of the Bible but literally the "parched land") is a dry region, much of it desert, which extends from south of Beer Sheba down to the Red Sea and the Sinai. Its mineral resources were mined by the ancients but are not considered economically exploitable today.

ABOVE: Beer Sheba (literally, "Well of the Covenant," as in Genesis 21:32) was the southern limit of the Promised Land (from Dan to Beer Sheba) and a noted sanctuary at the time of the Patriarchs: "And Abraham planted a grove in Beer-sheba, and called there on the name of the Lord, the everlasting God" (Genesis 21:33). A small Arab town until 1948, it became a new city when Israel was established and today has a population of two hundred thousand inhabitants. Pictured is the campus of the new Ben Gurion University of the Negev.

OPPOSITE: Elath is Israel's southernmost city on the shores of the Red Sea. There was nothing here in 1948 when Israel was established. The two dozen tin huts that stood here in 1950 have since become a port city of some fifty thousand inhabitants and a major winter and summer resort.

THESE PAGES: Over 1,900 years ago a remarkable people, the Nabateans, lived in the Negev Desert and successfully harnessed the perennial rivers in the wilderness. They developed agriculture in the harsh environment and built great cities such as Avdath (*left*). Aerial surveys have shown that hundreds of thousands of acres of desert land had been under cultivation by the Nabateans to support their relatively dense population. Modern farming in this area, as in Sde Boker (*above*), while using the latest achievements of agrotechnology, reapplies some of the sophisticated techniques of utilizing run-off waters first developed centuries ago by the Nabateans.

OVERLEAF: The tomb of David Ben-Gurion, Israel's first prime minister (*bottom right*) at Sde Boker, the desert kibbutz he joined after his retirement.

The Dead Sea: its level fluctuates, but at its median (1,300 feet below sea level) it is the lowest point on earth. Fed by the Jordan at its northernmost point, the Dead Sea has no exit. Its water is lost mainly through evaporation in the great heat. The evaporation produces a concentrated accumulation of mineral salts, making the sea almost ten times denser than ordinary sea water. It is possible to sit in the water and read a newspaper without sinking. Its mineral salts (mostly potassium chloride) are extracted by a Jordanian plant on its eastern shore and by an Israeli plant on its southern shore. In the fourth century B.C., the Egyptians imported bitumen from the Dead Sea for embalming their dead. The curative and other properties of Dead Sea salts exercised the imagination of ancient writers, from Aristotle to Pliny, Strabo, and Tacitus.

The Dead Sea and the Jordan River Valley together form part of the so-called Afro-Asian Rift, which reaches down south through the Red Sea as far as Kenya. The legend of Sodom and Gomorrah, traditionally located here at the southern end of the Dead Sea (*opposite*), may echo the distant cataclysm which brought the Afro-Asian Rift into being long before historical times. Genesis 19:24–25 says that "the Lord rained upon Sodom and Gemorrah brimstone and fire. . . . And he overthrew those cities, and all the plain."